A JOURNEY IN SEARCH OF JUSTICE

Confronting Ethical, Moral and
Professional Dilemmas in the Practice of Law

by
Stanley E. Tobin

Copyright, The Library of Congress
(Tx 815-409)
1997

Published by:
The Graduate Group
P.O. Box 370351
West Hartford, CT 06137-0351

A Journey in Search of Justice

TABLE OF CONTENTS

Chapter		Page
	Introduction	1
1	Forgive Them, Father, For They Know Not What They Do	5
2	One Flew Over The Apiary	13
3	The Wiley Lawyer	23
4	Lawyers in the Dock (Part I): The Rise and Decline of a Noble Profession	33
5	From Out of the West . . . The Lone Wranglers	45
6	Lawyers in the Dock (Part II): Raiders of the Lost Art	51
7	Judges on Trial: From Couch to Bench and Vice Versa	59
8	Airline I: Justice in Flight - Beyond the Wild Blue Ponder	73
9	Airline II: Justice Grounded -- Spaced Out	83
10	Clients -- O, Tempora! O, Mores!	89
11	Where There's A Will, There's A Gay	101

TABLE OF CONTENTS

Chapter		Page
12	Language and the Law: Of Slag and Slugs	111
13	Administration of the Law: Keeping Jeannie in the Bottle	123
14	The Counselor: Lettuce, Sit Down, and Reason Together	133
15	... Beyond Winning ... Vince Lombardi and Joe Kennedy Were Wrong	139
16	Justice -- More or Less	149
17	The JFK Assassination Miasma: A Conspiracy of Lawyers	165
18	Extra! Extra! The World's Not Fair	193
19	The World Of Our Fathers -- Ready-Mix Justice	203
20	"Let Us Raise A Somewhat Loftier Strain" (Virgil)	215

The strength of The Law is in its predictability, in the assurance that rights and property will be preserved and protected. But the beauty or wisdom of The Law is different; it is nurtured in uncertainty. In war an uncertain trumpet is dangerous. Off the battlefield, however, uncertainty reflects human nature and passion in an ever changing and enlightening world and society's always shifting moral standards. Strength and wisdom often vie -- each endures under the color of justice.

S.E.T.

Introduction

Lawyers, never strangers to criticism, today confront a crescendo of censure. The prestige and trust formerly accorded them are now at rock-bottom, while, paradoxically, their powers multiply, their ranks swell, and their incomes, though presently being reined in, remain embarrassingly high. Yet from within the profession itself, a once benign malaise has become pervasive. In this seemingly incongruous setting, we are witnessing radical changes in the practice of law, the way in which lawyers are perceived and judged, and the manner in which they view themselves. And in the troubling process, moral and professional standards and dilemmas, long indigenous to the practice of law, are often ignored or even frequently scorned.

The popular indictment against lawyers can no longer be taken lightly, least of all by the accused. While there is enough blame in today's warped legal processes to spread in all directions, lawyers must bear the brunt of the criticism. A Journey In Search of Justice seeks to lay out the case: Lawyers increasingly deserve much of the lashing and less of the fortune that is now accorded them. Not as a defense, but in mitigation of their failings, it must nonetheless be recognized that their ambition is to achieve often incompatible objectives -- ones which our overall society seldom reaches, let alone reconciles.

After almost forty years of practice, I still retain a genuine love and affection for the foundation and aims of the rule of law and due process and the paramount role that lawyers play in preserving and protecting these vital concepts. For a variety of reasons, however, this "magnificent undertaking" has become ever more disillusioning. Oliver Wendell Holmes, Jr., over a hundred years ago, described the lawyer's ordained plight as one where "he may wreak himself upon life, may drink the bitter cup of heroism, may wear his heart out after the unattainable." The moral and professional dilemmas of the past to which Holmes alluded have not diminished; rather, they have become exacerbated.

A Journey In Search of Justice, while not claiming to provide sure or many answers, aims to pose the problems in lifelike, everyday experiences that picture the profession in both its glory and its shame. The first chapter goes directly to the eye of the hurricane: American lawyers, entering the Twenty-First Century, are, ironically, uncertain as to what they actually <u>should</u> be doing and are ambivalent as to <u>how</u> they should be accomplishing often divergent goals.

Thereafter, I relate a dozen or so real cases and additional events and vignettes -- often commonplace travels -- that are hallmarks of the first third of my own professional practice. They present, however, a panoply of legal predicaments and puzzlements. These career experiences exemplify the present absence of direction and the uncertain underpinnings of the world's Second Oldest Profession. Taken and woven together, they, nonetheless, seek to bring the law to life and present both an exposition of the law to the layman and a meaning beyond materiality to the practitioner.

These frequently disconcerting stories aim to express an empathy for the profession, and, particularly, those within it who treat it as such, those who honestly confront the inherent moral and professional problems that demand, yet usually defy, ready answers. That the quest is time and again forlorn, if not quixotic, does not in the least diminish its importance.

Unlike many other books over the years on the practice and/or ills of lawyering, the stories that follow are not a collection of shopworn tales or grandiose triumphs. These chapters constitute, I believe, a critical appraisal of what lawyers do -- but, I write about them without rancor. Moreover, I recognize and appreciate society's leeriness of the legal process in general, and lawyers in particular -- but, I am not unmindful about and make no apologia for the public's misuse of both the process and its practitioners. And, on the whole, I maintain a healthy respect for the judges who must, under the most trying circumstances, act Solomon-like amidst disintegrating temples -- but, given their human frailties, no paean is appropriate.

These integrated stories and reminiscences should tell lawyers and laymen more about each other in a fashion that may help bring us together. I seek to follow a path similar to that which Addison outlined for himself in The Spectator papers almost 300 years ago. "It was said of Socrates," Addison wrote, "that he brought philosophy down from heaven to inhabit among men; and I shall be ambitious to have it said about me that I have brought philosophy out of the closets and libraries, schools and colleges, to dwell in clubs and assemblies, at tea-tables, and in coffee-houses." "Lawyering" must not be cloistered in the courthouses. To survive in a meaningful sense, it must be exposed to and understood by those in the coffeehouses.[1]

---

[1] These stories serve another, if secondary, purpose. Henry James said it so nicely in the preface to the chapter on Venice in his Italian Hours:

> "It is a great pleasure to write the word, but I am not sure there is not a certain impudence in pretending to add anything to it . . . There is nothing new to be said . . . I do not pretend to enlighten the reader; I pretend only to give a fillip to his memory; and I hold any writer sufficiently justified who is himself in love with his theme."

Every attorney has a repertoire of cases that he expounds for his own purposes. This is mine.

Chapter 1.

Forgive Them, Father, For
They Know Not What They Do

1986 was more than an unusual year in legal circles -- it was surrealistic. For over a decade, the youth of America of all races and creeds and from all walks of life were storming the law schools and causing an explosive growth in the number of practicing lawyers; and this surge was slated to continue for at least another decade. Yet, all this was being accompanied by deep disillusionment within and wide-spread disparagement from without the profession.

Now, after still another decade in the throes of this paradox, despite many attorneys still in denial, the evidence and authorities are overwhelmingly in accord: the profession is being shattered by a multitude of ills. There is a general consensus as to the causes, although disagreement exists as to the emphasis to be given to each of the many recognized symptoms (some of which are hopefully brought to life in the experiences related in the chapters that follow).

Many of the culprits are perennial pests now grown more daring; others are a new breed of bacteria. A few are self-induced afflictions. Some -- probably including the most virulent -- reflect the (changing) society which gives birth to, weans and nurtures the legal community. In reality, leading the malaise-list factors that have caused the current sturm und drang within the profession is the nature of today's society itself.

In the words of the Okefenokee philosopher: "we have met the enemy and they is us." This nation, and Western society in general, are being victimized by their own democratic and material success -- a success that has been heralded and highlighted by rapid and pervasive communication, totally unimagined less than a half-century ago. This, we now know, has led to an insatiable demand by more and more for more and more; now, not later. Rights, not duties, is the escutcheon. Advocates, not counsellors, legal technicians, not "lawyer-statesmen" are now sought out. And the "profession," which in our democracy has always represented the vox populi, has willingly yielded to the tide.

Accompanying this "entitlement demand," the increased complexity of the law itself, the need for evermore specialization amidst a technological revolution, expanding populations and court calendars, have almost tripled the number of attorneys in scarcely a score of years. In the wake of this explosion, lawyers, in turn, have abandoned elitism and are losing loyalty to once venerable firms as well as trust from and confidante relationships with clients. We are no longer stunned to witness daily "trial by press" conferences sponsored by opposing counsel, nor astonished to read about law firms retaining PR firms on a permanent, profit-sharing basis. Rather than acting as peer responsible guardians to each other, as they had in the past, in this caldron of chaos many a lawyer instead has become incredibly creative in conducting costly paper wars and opening new orifices in his opponent's corpus. Chummy camaraderie was not in years past always the profession's hallmark, but today's "in your face" climate would have been anathema.

This entire parade of horribles is now well documented and understood nationwide by most of the bench and bar, but that has not slowed down the seemingly inexorable lemming march to reach the lowest common denominator. In 1986, however, the alarm bell, belatedly, began to ring. The ABA convention that year in New York unintentionally highlighted its enfeebling conundrum. Depicting this state of schizophrenia, thousands of successful lawyers attended such seminars as "How To Build A Million Dollar Practice" or sat glued to their seats in another seminar entitled "Marketing Legal Services." In this latter session the lawyers were told bluntly by a California attorney and author that, "There's not enough business out there for all of you." Some of the tips advocated to meet this pending Gotterdammerung sounded, as the Wall Street Journal remarked, "suspiciously like ... hustling." In the past ten years, the number of such seminars has skyrocketed -- many of them on chartered cruises to Europe and elsewhere, tax-deductible.

At the very time that these and other shenanigans were going on, these same lawyers, in mind-boggling juxtaposition, met and bemoaned the state of the profession as portrayed by a then recent report of the ABA's Commission on Professionalism. The Report asserted that the "temptation" of attorneys to "put profits first" is greater than at any other time in history. The ABA's membership wrestled with its rhetorical conclusion: "Has our profession abandoned principle for profit, professionalism for commercialism?" Whatever the angst was then, in the years since the problem has become painfully worse.

This cry against commercialism has not been limited to our shores. In England and other Western democracies the attack against the "silks" has become unprecedentedly vocal and widespread. London's attorneys are pricing themselves on par with their colleagues in the Colonies. Indeed, in 1997, in calling for reform, in his first public act, the new Labour Government's Lord Chancellor denounced (in words somewhat less cricket than Lord Chesterfield would have chosen) the "fat cat lawyers" of Her Majesty's realm. Universally, attorneys -- the front-line, elitist protectors of the Rule of Law -- have become modern Praetorian Guards (or are at least being so viewed, and with disdain).

The single question the ABA Report posed encompassed only part of the problem -- the business end or bottom-line factor. It, and innumerable other studies for over a century, gingerly addressed this money-making aspect of lawyering. It is as though its disclosure is faintly confessional in nature and it is usually accompanied with the plea that practitioners of the art should be granted indulgence, if not absolution, for having to soil their hands in this otherwise worthy undertaking. Balderdash! The practice of law has always been, in very large part, a business. The industrial and technological eras have made it even more so and the informational age now fully exposes this down-to-earth realty. The practice of law in this and the next millennium is not an eleemosynary enterprise.

Only, however, when the self-aggrandizement becomes blatant and pronounced, when the "business" significantly compromises the moral and ethical standards that are the bulwark of the profession, does society in general and the profession itself become tarnished and endangered. Unfortunately, we have reached at least the outskirts of that dismal destination.

A second part of the problem commands special attention. To some extent this other factor is even more vexing, for it goes to the very core of the problem -- the <u>raison d'être</u> of the profession. What is the main role of the lawyer? His purpose? To serve justice or the client? Is he primarily an "officer of the court" or a partisan-advocate for the client? As might be expected, few other legal subjects have been discussed at greater length than this most basic of all considerations surrounding the plight of the profession. And hardly surprising, these vital questions are themselves troublesome, the answers elusive and divisive. The profession, consequently, is increasingly encased in a state of debilitating ambivalence.

Prompted by the ABA's 1986 "call to arms," attorney groups throughout the country began to parley in an effort to meet that challenge. The remarkable disarray that encircles the profession on the quintessential issue as to the lawyers' principal purpose was pointedly exposed at a 1989 conclave of California lawyers held in Los Angeles. There, some 38 leading attorneys, judges and members of the Establishment met at what was billed as a "pioneering assembly focused on . . . discussing the meaning of professionalism applied to the practice of law." These quite successful practitioners were in overwhelming accord as to the predicament of the profession. Similar agreement, however, was far less attainable as to whether certain fairly routine types of lawyers' conduct should be considered ethically acceptable. On many such ethical and moral issues, covering both run-of-the-mill and serious practices, those elite attorneys expressed significant disagreement and/or uncertainty.

This divisiveness/unsureness on the part of the bar is, upon reflection, understandable. Essentially, it emanates from the astonishing disagreement and ambivalence lawyers have as to their role in society. These California lawyers were asked to respond to 25 written propositions involving common but troublesome legal dilemmas by indicating their agreement or disagreement as to the proper course of action that should be taken to each of them. Almost all of their answers were obviously affected by two critical questions which were included in the very middle of the questionnaire. When asked whether "a lawyer's primary obligation is to serve his client," 32 attorneys responded. Every one of them had an opinion. Twenty-nine of them agreed or strongly agreed with that statement. Only three disagreed. Then these same attorneys and judges responded to the very next question which was whether "a lawyer's primary obligation is to uphold the system of justice." Obviously, this is quite different, frequently inconsistent and often diametrically opposite to the prior proposition. Nonetheless, 29 of the same esteemed practitioners, all of whom again having a definite opinion, answered as follows: Twenty-six of them agreed or strongly agreed with this statement. Three (perhaps the only consistent ones) disagreed. Magically, these skilled men and women of the law had, with apparent equanimity, inserted a square peg into a round hole.

Lawyers, of course, have been eternally and caustically accused of arguing opposite sides of the same issue. Guilty as charged. That is a proper and understandable professional prerequisite. To do so, however, on the very same occasion and on what goes to the essence of the profession's purpose seems to defy the gods and to suggest either extraordinary mental agility or sublimity encroaching on stupidity. This barrister abracadabra can only cause further confusion and cynicism on the part of the layman.

But wait. The lawyer's uncertain trumpet does not escape the sensitive antennae of the thoughtful and impressionable lay witness. Take Holden Caulfield, for instance. About fifty years ago, he like most young idealists, yearned to make his life meaningful, to become a savior to those in need, to be a catcher in the rye. Why not become a lawyer like his father, suggested his sister. To which Holden replied:

> "Lawyers are all right, I guess--but it doesn't appeal to me. I mean they're all right if they go around saving innocent guys' lives all the time, and like that, but you don't *do* that kind of stuff if you're a lawyer. All you do is make a lot of dough and play golf and play bridge and buy cars and drink Martinis and look like a hot-shot. And besides. Even if you *did* go around saving guys' lives and all, how would you know if you did it because you really *wanted* to save guys' lives, or because you did it because what you *really* wanted to do was be a terrific lawyer, with everybody slapping you on the back and congratulating you in court when

the goddam trial was over, the reporters and everybody, the way it is in the dirty movies? How would you know you weren't being a phony? The trouble is, you *wouldn't*."

Holden, who didn't quite get it correct in quoting Robert Burns ("If a body <u>meet</u> a body coming through the rye"), was "right on" in understanding lawyers. As far as he was concerned they not only didn't know what they were doing, but even if they did, they wouldn't know why they were doing it.

Yet, those attorneys meeting in Los Angeles did the best they could as they squirmed in no-win quicksand. The practice is not monolithic. For, in the final analysis, there are in reality four factors which often pull in four different directions and that serve to quarter lawyers, even those with the best intentions: "professionalism" versus commercialism ("business") versus partisan advocate (The Client) versus justice. These living concepts are very often in tension and vie with each other, and yet, they constitute the Four Foundations of a lawyer's career. All of them must be taken into consideration and each has, at times, some measure of priority. Still, the search for justice, the first among equals, must take the lead. It is the North Star.

Each of the legal cases and career challenges portrayed in this book reveals one or more of the moral and professional dilemmas posed by these Four Foundations. They are of the same type as those always present, pesky problems that confounded those elite members of the Los Angeles bar. Some lurk beneath the surface; others confront us starkly. But whether they appear by whisper or wail, they should command our attention. The way they are handled changes the destiny of all of us.

Holden Caulfield probably never became an attorney, but if he had he would now be looking toward retirement and would likely be more sympathetic as to what a lawyer does and the difficult load an honorable lawyer bears. A lawyer just <u>might</u> be "all right" (with appropriate apologies to both Kipling and Burns):

If he realizes the profits of his business, but knows that his aim must encompass a great deal more;

If he treats his profession as a chalice to be handed down with pride, not as a platform to display pride;

If he considers his clients above himself, but not the law;

If he recognizes that it is often a will-o'the-wisp, but always gives <u>justice</u> the nod;

Then, when the day nears its end and he has filed his last appeal, he can hold his head up a little higher . . . when that lawyer meet a lawyer coming through the mire.

Chapter 2.

One Flew Over The Apiary

It was the early summer of 1959. I had been in practice only two or three weeks. I was 28 years old, with the best in formal education behind me and seemingly unlimited opportunity beckoning me. My then-specialty, condemnation law, was having a statutory facelift as directed by the California legislature, and I was one of the plastic surgeons. This, despite the fact that I had absolutely no practical experience in that or, for that matter, any other area of the law. At that time and place this was, at most, a mild handicap.

On that day, however, my mind was not absorbed with lofty, or even mundane, musings. I was in the office law library, performing the necessary drudgery of all young attorneys -- grinding through gray-toned books; this was long before the age of the computerized search, the laser lawyer. I was with the firm (the bottom line on the letterhead) with which I have now worked for my entire professional career. Initially, I mainly did a great deal of academic writing in condemnation law, but with the enticing opportunity to handle as diverse and as heavy a caseload in all fields as would be available.

One of the senior partners, somehow thinking that the Boston Latin School of itself created gifted lawyers, encouraged me to seize the reins of the practice as quickly as possible, engage in litigation from the very start, and act as though I knew it all from the outset. Among his other attributes, he was the legal community's connection with the Church. As such, he was bestowed with the power, as a layman, to tear asunder the things that God had brought together, that is, cases referred quietly by Church functionaries to civil attorneys to do that which the Church itself cannot do -- smooth the way for divorce. From time to time this attorney, a wise counselor, would in his professional capacity act as the attorney for one spouse or the other to gain a divorce from the bonds of matrimony at the behest of some unknown personage in the Church. The latter, having reviewed the facts, recognized that legally an annulment was not available and the doctrine of abstention was not necessarily God's will.

Around ten o'clock that morning, the telephone in my legal cubicle rang. I was told by my Church-connected colleague that he was then tied up in ongoing day and nightlong labor negotiations. Would I be so kind as to get the file in <u>Morales v. Morales</u> and appear in the Superior Court in Santa Ana, some thirty-five miles away, at 2:00 p.m. to handle a domestic relations case for our client, Angela Morales. It wasn't really a question; it was a command. I am sure that thousands of young attorneys over the course of time have received their first cases under similar circumstances, knowing nothing about the case, directed to handle it, and presented the file but hours beforehand. At that time, however, I innocently thought my situation was almost unique, and I took the assignment with awe and challenge. I arranged to meet my client an hour before court time to prepare her for a contested divorce action.

Two things need be understood about the practice of divorce law in the late 1950's and 1960's until it was changed in 1970. First, it was necessary to prove fault, that is, that one spouse or the other had broken the moral code that existed at the time and therefore he or she could be sanctimoniously tarred and feathered. Since 1970 we have supposedly become more civilized; fault need not (cannot) be shown. That civility, however, is more theory than practice; and to the extent that it exists at all, it prevails primarily because society cannot sacrifice the time, effort and money to determine "fault." Fault, moreover, often hovers in the twilight zone, the transitory. Indeed, the criteria for yesterday's fault often provide the formulae for today's success.

So "fault" went the way of all flesh, if you will. But the legal result is frequently form over substance. Wherever children are involved, fault, one way or another, will creep in when the belligerent parting partners cannot amicably resolve their differences. Children now may actually be used as weapons, even more so than in the past. Furthermore, a whole variety of camouflaged fault factors are entertained by the courts, often in a seeming effort to seek something called equity. The subtlest product of "fault" (A's) is "equity" (B's). But fault was then a direct and necessary, indeed vital, factor to be proven and I had to prove it or my client would lose either a satisfactory amount of support or what is often quaintly called "community property." She could even be defaulted. Not a favorable omen in the first case of one's promising career.

A second factor that I was to be confronted with was the Family Law Department, called the "divorce court" in normal parlance. It had, and still has in large part, all the physical and emotional ambience of a Hogarth picture of Bedlam. Daumier and Dickens come alive. Children crawling under benches, emotionally wounded, feigning insouciance and pleading innocence, trying to hide hurt and cover up shame, dragged into the cold corridors of the court, a vision etched forever in their minds, returning for years predictably and periodically to haunt them. Dragooned there because there is no other place to leave them, or because one or both parents needs shields or seconds, or lawyers need exhibits, or judges "insight." And the warring parents, in some ways even more vulnerable. They can't hide under the benches.

Litigants, both men and women, searching for attorneys they have scarcely, if ever, met; attorneys searching for clients whose names are listed in their files. Bailiffs shouting out the names of litigants, witnesses and lawyers as though everyone was in a crowded lost-and-found department. Men hauled in, barely cognizant as to how they got into such a place or predicament and even less sure how they would get out of such straits. Women having nothing left to look forward to but fear, and terrorized by the future. The overwhelming emotion is the endless finality of it all. Lawyers strutting about as if they owned the place -- highly paid and haughty padrones. Calendars overcrowded, judges soporifically calling the roll, reflecting a resignation and frustration at the summariness of it all.

But I was young and spirited and did not let such visions dull my sense of mission. So I opened up the file and read the documents attached to the complaint that had been filed some weeks before. I then realized that I was representing a relatively young woman with two daughters, ages 8 and 9, against a man who, from the legalese language of the complaint, had expressed amorous inklings towards someone other than his wife. More importantly, he also was too amorous, in his own way, towards his wife. The reader should know that despite my education I was about as square as anyone from Boston could be; that is, ill-equipped to handle this case. I was better qualified to be an astronaut! Indeed, I was somewhat mystified as to what the husband had really done and I intended to pursue the matter with my client at the first opportunity, which was a little more than two hours away.

But I had an interim assignment, one that would tax the most accomplished lawyer. It seemed that the defendant's trade was

Dear Friend:

If, for some enigmatic reason, you desire an additional copy of <u>A Journey In Search Of Justice</u>, you may call or write me before September 15, 1998 and I'll arrange it being sent to you at the cost price of $12.00. Thereafter, you can get copies through the publisher at its probable price of $17.95, plus mailing.

            SET

<u>New address as of June 15, 1998</u>:

One California Plaza
300 South Grand Avenue, 37th Floor
Los Angeles, CA 90071-3147
(213) 620-0460/Fax: (213) 624-4840

owning, tending, and producing a profit from apiaries. I scarcely knew what an apiary was. But now I had an assignment to obtain from the court an order to divide the apiaries as community property. Just how do you go about that? Dammit, they hadn't taught me that in law school.

Frantically, I searched in every imaginable way to ascertain how I could get the court to divide these bee-hives, literally hundreds of them, sprawled across miles and miles of hot desert, some but not all tagged by numbers, some but not all containing honey, and all too many of them occupied by an active queen and thousands of drones, doing their thing. I needed an order prepared for the court that would both evaluate these hives, queens and all, and permit the sheriff to attach them if necessary, indemnity and all.

In and out of the <u>Corpus Juris Secundum</u>, rifling through the Civil Code and the Code of Civil Procedure, up and down the ALR, through the digests, beaver-like I advanced, the picture of a knowledgeable lawyer, seeking a case on point. Frustratingly, for apparent naught. Only at the last minute, just before I had to speed off to the court, by sheer chance I came across the only case on point! It discussed at some length how the sheriff was to attach and take possession and account for apiaries in a similar situation. This sole authority, ruefully, was an English case in 1593! Still, authority is authority and I shot off to the Santa Ana courthouse like a barrister, acting as though through years of erudition he had easily put his finger upon the case directly on the mark. The kind of look that I was to adopt honestly -- only occasionally thereafter.

Just before leaving for court, I put in a telephone call to my client about where I would meet her and had the presence of mind to inform her that I did not want her two children to come to court. I met her about 25 minutes before court was to convene. The halls of the Family Law Department, marble and clean, new and sparkling, light and spacious, nonetheless had the awful ambience of family failure, a place, in the mind at least, so depressing that coping with the vision itself exhausts the participants. Stockyard justice. Heaven's veneer cannot hide the here and now Hell.

In these surroundings of magnificent foreboding I met my client, an attractive and intelligent woman about my age. She appeared strong but at the edge of shatterdom. In no time I realized that she was as guilt-ridden as anybody I had ever met. I made it quite plain to her from the start that it was unlikely that any judge would give her all that she asked for in the complaint, and that the "pie" would almost surely be more equally divided. Fortunately, she recognized the axiom of necessity. After going over the complaint with her and realizing how difficult it would be for her to obtain, as the complaint prayed, $450 of her husband's $610 monthly take-home pay, I nonetheless was convinced that her expenses and the need to support her children justified that prayer and could be supported by the evidence.

Satisfied that she would respond to my questions in a satisfactory manner on this principal issue, I then turned my attention to that nasty little concept called "fault." What indeed had Richard Morales done? It was clear to me, even in my naivete, that Mrs. Morales was still very much in love with him and would rather be marrying than divorcing him. Plainly holding back tears and perhaps sensing *my* hesitation, she began to explain why she (or was it the Church?) felt it necessary that a divorce be had. I gleaned that Richard had picked up an odd habit of coming home from work and, not merely desiring sexual relations in the missionary manner, had sought -- and received for approximately ten years -- sexual satisfaction by a method often described as being the downfall of Sodom and Gomorrah. Yes, there was no escape; this conduct was so legally verboten that in the law books and statutes it could be described only in veiled (if piquant) terms such as "the abominable crime against Nature" or with the acronym TACAN. When I realized the nature of "fault" I did not know whether to laugh or cringe, but I knew I would have difficulty in presenting it to the court. But courts are wise, and I reassured myself that the sensitivity of my problem would be alleviated by the court's compassion.

This impression was embodied in a judge who looked more fit for his role than Warren Burger and Earl Warren combined. Judge James Kingbe Wright was a legend in his time, as was his father in his time (who was also a judge). The epitome of the Establishment, the cornerstone of the law, and, fortunately or otherwise, a centurion of rectitude.

The years since 1959 cover little more than a third of a century. Time, however, cannot be measured by years alone. From 1959 to today is approximately 2-1/2 eons, as compared with the hundred years from 1859 to 1959. There has been no time in recorded history when change has been so rapid. And Alvin Toffler was certainly on the mark in describing this revolutionary change and its consequences in the element of time as it applies to the period since 1959.

At any rate, with the form of assurance that defies logic but not youth, I undertook to present my case. It was first necessary for me to prove fault. My client testified as to the marriage, and then I edged towards the arena of wickedness. In response to my gingerly worded questions, it became reasonably apparent, even to devotees of Louisa May Alcott, that Mrs. Morales had been compelled to engage in a sexual practice which at that time, according to the Penal Code of the State of California, was a crime. In my direct examination of her, I brought everything into focus except Henry Miller.

Satisfied that I had performed this delicate examination with professional class, I nevertheless thought it advisable to get confirmation from the court that I had met the legal requirement. Turning to the judge, I respectfully stated, "Your Honor, I believe that I have established fault satisfactorily so that I can go on to the division of property and support." The judge, tilting his head and unfurling his distinguished gray mane, looked down upon this novitiate attorney and replied, "Counsel, this is your case. I am not going to help you out. It is for you to initially decide the question as to whether you have proven fault. I will reserve my decision on that issue."

I was dumbfounded! That powerful man, sitting on his throne in those intimidating black robes -- the habit of authority -- was in effect counseling me to choose between quite possibly being non-suited or instead opening up for the record, for her shame, for her husband's mortification, for my unease and for a confused and troubled courtroom audience, all the detailed entails of conjugal life. All for what purpose?

Chagrined, I turned my back to the judge in a show of not-so-subtle contempt towards the court, stared out at the few people sitting in the benches, and realized that of course some of them were the parties' parents. I swung around and said, "Your Honor, at least do me the favor of clearing the courtroom." In a sense of benign accommodation, he responded, "That I will do for you, counsel." And so he ordered. I then went into the lurid details while the parties fidgeted before the seemingly stoic judge.

Having concluded this knotty business, I turned my examination of my client to the questions of support and the division of community property (of which there was scarcely any), and I believe I was fairly professional in demonstrating her clear need. Soon afterwards, the defendant husband, somewhat anticipating his preordained doom, testified as to his need, which I felt was fair. After all, even in 1959 his need for $75 a week did not seem exorbitant. He never met the issue of fault, and I felt no need to cross-examine him.

Judge Wright excused himself and went into his chambers. He soon returned from his secular Sistine Chapel, strode up to the bench, and enunciated that he had reached a decision. He began by summarily stating, as a matter of fact, that the plaintiff had proven that the defendant was at fault. After granting uncontested custody of the children to my client, he then divided up the small amount of community property. He then proceeded to order the sale of the apiaries in accordance with the 1593 formula that I had forwarded.

At the conclusion, he reached the heart of the matter, saying "The plaintiff's prayer in her complaint of $450 a month in support for herself and the children in the manner sought is appropriate, and I am ordering the defendant to pay such amount each month." At that moment Richard Morales, realizing the paltry sum left to him to support himself, going to and from work and trying to live his life, jumped up, ignoring his own counsel, and literally screamed to the court, "Your Honor, how can I possibly live on $160 a month?" To which the judge replied in a cool, carefully modulated tone, "Young man, for ten years you have been unzipping your fly; now tighten your belt."

I froze in disbelief. As gratified as I was for the moment with my "victory" in this, my first case, the court's stinging remark was too unsettling to savor triumph. The proceeding soon concluded. I spoke briefly with my client; she told me how much she appreciated my work and that she knew the Church would be pleased as well. Aimlessly, I drove back to Los Angeles. I wallowed back into the firm's offices, carrying my briefcases like Willy Loman. I walked dazedly down the corridor to the office library and spotted one of the middle-aged associates who had been practicing for some years. "Al," I said, somewhat sheepishly, "what do you do when a judge gives the wife and kids $450 a month and the husband takes home only $610 a month?" Al looked at me and said, matter-of-factly, "Appeal!" I replied, "How can I appeal? <u>I won</u>!"

* * * * *

I do not know what ever happened to the Moraleses. Whether Dick was able to cope with his "sentence" to an indefinite term in the poorhouse is an inquiry lost in history. Did he pay the alimony and support ordered? Probably not. Just another statistic, proving for sure, that most ex-husbands and fathers are deadbeats, no-accounts, justice-defying wastrels.

If I was to be mystified, indeed disturbed, by the power of the Always Wrights and their conscious and unconscious methods of enforcing their own codes of conduct and morality, or defining and then enforcing right-and wrong and hiding what they were doing from themselves and society behind robes that are appropriately black, I also came to realize that lawyers could lawyer in a way to appeal to those human hang-ups, to the ends or end of justice. The consequences of such a process cause an unease, a disturbing shadow that follows any thoughtful lawyer in and out of the courthouses throughout his career.

Chapter 3.

__The Wiley Lawyer__

Abraham Lincoln was, by most measurements, a successful attorney. He was not, however, a student of the law nor even studious in his effort and approach to the practice. Yet, he had one dominant characteristic in pursuing and performing his profession. That characteristic was, in its adamant adherence, unusual then and is probably even more so today -- he considered that he had no higher duty than to seek a just and fair result. He owed his client no more, himself no less. Repeatedly, he would reject his own client's claims if he felt they were unfair or overreaching, regardless of their legality.

One such telling example was related to William Herndon, Lincoln's law partner and famous biographer. In an undated manuscript sent to Herndon after Lincoln's death, the author wrote:

> "One morning, not long before Lincoln's nomination -- a year perhaps -- I was in your

[Herndon's] office and heard the following: Mr. Lincoln, seated at the baize-covered table in the center of the office, listened attentively to a man who talked earnestly and in a low tone. After being thus engaged for some time Lincoln at length broke in, and I shall never forget his reply. 'Yes,' he said, 'we can doubtless gain your case for you; we can set a whole neighborhood at loggerheads; we can distress a widowed mother and her six fatherless children and thereby get for you six hundred dollars to which you seem to have a legal claim, but which rightfully belongs, it appears to me, as much to the woman and her children as it does to you. You must remember that some things legally right are not morally right. We shall not take your case, but will give you a little advice for which we will charge you nothing. You seem to be a sprightly, energetic man; we would advise you to try your hand at making six hundred dollars some other way.'" (Abraham Lincoln, by William H. Herndon and Jesse W. Weik, Vol- 2, pp. 14-15, D. Appleton and Company, New York and London, 1920)

The clarity and fastidiousness of this, his overriding tenet, made Lincoln even in his own time, among his peers, a distinguished lawyer. Today, many believe this trait remarkable, almost unique; some consider it inappropriate, even wrong.

* * * * *

Lincoln may have pungently enunciated the true role of the lawyer in society. The road to Damascus, however, is not usually so straight nor nearly so clear. Moral ambiguities are repeatedly confronted along the way. One such encounter for me came about two years after a stung Dick Morales learned the facts of life. In 1961, I accepted what was the last divorce case I would ever handle -- thank God.[2] Again I prevailed. But again, at least in retrospect, triumph was accompanied by a gnawing concern, a disconcerting doubt. Just how elastic is the lawyer's license?

A likable 68 year old roustabout by the name of Wiley Beatty walked into my office one morning. Without describing it as anything more than another of life's vicissitudes, he related his plight and asked if I would represent him. Wiley was the prototypal "regular" American guy -- wiry, tough, feisty, and perpetually optimistic. A product of much of that generation born at the turn of the century, he was an endless wanderer and a hard worker, a self-made man (to the extent that is possible) who felt that America was about the best thing in the world.

Along the way, he had three wives. And a temper. At least the latter usually got the better of him. His first wife, back in Missouri, divorced him because he literally kicked her around too much. His second mate, to whom he had been married for about five years, successfully sued him and virtually wiped him out, when a court awarded her the few thousand dollars he then had. Wiley had made the mistake of shooting her. Actually, I believed him when he said he had loved her but just didn't appreciate her playing around. Following that marital debacle, he again started saving as much as he could, looking forward to quitting the drilling rigs and going "back home" to spend his remaining years

---

[2]The divorce case just before the one related here fittingly happened in Hollywood and afforded a moment of comic relief. Representing Lucy Felizi, I had easily undone her defendant husband on cross-examination. So much so that when he was leaving the witness stand, he asked for my card! I was never again to receive such a compliment. A few minutes later I was to witness an even more surprising turn of events. Despite the adverse monetary decision he had just received and the pronouncement of divorce on both of them, the parties not only waltzed out of the courtroom arm in arm and cheek to cheek, but they were actually embracing. As I watched them through the glass courtroom doors rush away together, I would have taken bets they were beginning their honeymoon! Amo, amas, amaretto.

if not whittling away on pieces of wood, at least continuing to hunt and barhop; or perhaps they were one and the same.

But Wiley, rough and ready as always, soon became lonely again; and his loneliness could be assuaged only by Ima, who he met at a bar, hunting. First the hair; then the teeth; last the illusions.

Ima, as he depicted her and as I later verified on meeting her, was what one might describe, in the terminology of the time, as a "tough broad." Divorced after a brief marriage many years before, she was diminutive and soft-spoken, true, but nonetheless tough. According to Wiley, Ima was well aware of his temper and aware of her own needs for the future. She was in her early 60s, a nurse who would soon retire and who had, as the only income ahead of her, Social Security. She seemingly took Mozart's musical ditty literally: Love is like a little thief. Wiley believed that he had been "set up." I think he was right, though of course, as far as I know, he had sight in both of his eyes.

As Wiley described it to me, during their six stormy years of holy gridlock, Ima constantly egged him on, causing his temper to display itself in its usual ornery manner. "She knew exactly what would upset me," Wiley would repeat, "and she insisted on getting me upset. She <u>wanted</u> me to hit her." And he obliged. "Yes," he told me, "I hit her a number of times, and she has got this lawyer and wants to take the $8,500 I have, which I set aside for my retirement to go home to Missouri. Her lawyer says she is going to get it all. Can you help me, sir?"

I liked Wiley, not only because of the cut of his jib, but because I felt he was telling me the truth. He certainly was down-to-earth, with no apparent guile. He did not hem and haw and he did not downplay his temper, nor did he cuss Ima. Wiley was not exactly Gary Cooper, though he had some of his attributes. He just wanted a fair share, and was willing to fight for it. Indeed, he was the first and last client to pay my entire fee in advance, in cash -- $200, mainly in one dollar bills!

But how to get Wiley out of the hole he had dug for himself was to be no easy task. In 1961 California, as almost all other states, was still in the dungeons of "fault" divorce. Most times, fault divorce meant the following: (1) judges like James Kingsbe Wright would have their day made; (2) penny-catching newspapers would sell papers that their general readership would actually read; (3) lawyers could make a courtroom a stage for the scandalous; and (4) one spouse or the other (or both) could be reduced to ignominy, financially and personally. Thirty-five years later, in the era of no-fault divorce, some of this savage approach to human problems had been alleviated, but unfortunately most of this sewage still percolates in practice.

No question about it, in front of a judge, Ima Beatty would be able to "prove" that Wiley was a scoundrel who had long inflicted great bodily harm and trauma to this delicate little old lady. And the Old Testament disjunctive would come into play: there would be no turning the other cheek, but there would be "an eye for an eye." Since that could not literally be done (the Hammurabi Code was no longer viable, even assuming it had ever applied to overly assertive husbands),[3] Wiley would make his amends to society by turning over to Ima his life savings. Wiley was too honest a

---

[3]The only possible relevant provisions of that Code seem to apply to women other than wives:

> "§ 209 If a man has struck a free woman with child, and has caused her to miscarry, he shall pay ten shekels for her miscarriage.
>
> § 210 If that woman die, his daughter shall be killed.
>
> § 211 If it be the daughter of a plebeian, that has miscarried through his blows, he shall pay five shekels of silver.
>
> § 212 If that woman die, he shall pay half a mina of silver."

witness, I thought, simply to deny, in a convincing fashion, that he had done these things. Even if I entertained his doing so, there was no question that Ima would undoubtedly have a witness or two to the dastardly acts. And old Wiley certainly could not wipe out the records in his prior divorce cases, which a competent lawyer probably would be able to get into evidence one way or another. No question about it, Appleton's First Rule of L.A. Law would come into play: a guy with a temper is a goner.

It was a neat setup. Ima did it beautifully. Perhaps not diabolically or even consciously. But at some point there was the realization that she "had" him. From that moment on, Wiley's goose was inexorably tied to his gander's timing.

Wiley had to be saved despite himself, and I knew of no way to save him in court. I spent two or three restless evenings conjuring up ways in which I could, in Clarence Darrow fashion, turn the tables. The next morning I concluded that it could not be done that way. Once more I called Wiley into my office to go over the facts. In the course of our conferences, Wiley, as with all clients, had mentioned a number of things which were either immaterial, irrelevant, unintelligible, or not very interesting. What most lawyers do is separate what is important from what is not. And one thing he happened to mention, which certainly did not appear to be important, was that Ima Rosedale Beatty was not really her name. Apparently, Wiley said, she had been born in Wisconsin and Rosedale was not her father's name. It was an adoptive name. Hardly anyone, after all these years, knew that. Wiley had found out only recently, by pure chance. Ima was extremely careful not to reveal it to anyone, including Wiley.

Ima apparently was a bastard in more than one way. But so what! Here it was 62 years later, a world apart and a divorce case wherein Ima's legitimacy was about as relevant as Catherine the Great's chastity. So I discarded that little morsel of information. Yet as the days and weeks went on, I still could not piece together a case for mercy.

Then it happened. How it came to mind and fell together is one of those inexplicable happenstances; no matter how we try logically to piece together the train of thought that brings a matter to culmination, it simply defies logical analysis. Only in retrospect was it obvious.

Surely as plain as the nose on my face, if Ima was illegitimate and was as uptight about it as Wiley suggested, she probably would not tell <u>anyone</u> -- not even her lawyer. And if her lawyer knew about it, he would think nothing of it because it was irrelevant! But Ima didn't know it was irrelevant! And she would not raise the point of relevance even to-her lawyer. Deep wounds never heal; they just cover up and turn to steel. It requires a bypass to be able to live comfortably with them.

The next week I was scheduled to take Ima's deposition in the conference room of my firm. There was little I could learn that I had not already learned from Wiley and from the responses to the interrogatories I had sent out. From the description of Ima given to me by Wiley, I had no doubt that this was a shrewd woman unlikely to give any quarter, or dollar. Nonetheless, having stirred this strategy and the tactics around in my mind for a few days, I called Wiley and told him I wanted him to be in an adjacent room when I took Ima's deposition. Normally this would be entirely unnecessary, but I believed the arrangement would be helpful in this instance. When Ima and her attorney arrived, I advised them that Wiley was in the next room, and from time to time during the deposition I left to confer with him, with Ima being aware of that.

I started the deposition by asking, naturally, her name. "Ima Beatty," she replied. "Your full name, please." "Ima Rosedale Beatty." "Is Rosedale your maiden name?" She paused and then said, a bit hesitantly, "Why, yes." "So Rosedale was your maiden name?" She paused again and then responded in a low tone, "Yes." "And prior to your marriage to Mr. Beatty, you were known all your life, except during your prior marriage, as Ima

Rosedale, is that correct?" She looked at me strangely and said, "Yes."

I then went on to all sorts of other things. About a half-hour later in the course of the deposition, after leaving the room ostensibly to talk to my client, I resumed and said, "By the way, what did you say your maiden name was again?" Her lawyer showed no interest in the question, but Ima appeared a bit perturbed and replied, with a little edge in her voice, "As I said, it was Rosedale." "Oh, so you did."

About one hour later, I had finished all the questions I could pose to her. Her lawyer seemed perfectly satisfied that Ima had done a fine job, but Ima seemed ill at ease, and she became further distracted when I concluded my examination by saying "Oh, just one final question. I am correct in saying, am I not, Mrs. Beatty, that your maiden name, the name you were born with, is Rosedale?" I said this as though I had merely had a lapse of memory. Ima answered with obvious and uncomfortable restraint, in the affirmative. I then declared that I had no further questions, the deposition was over, and I would see her and her lawyer at trial. After a few long seconds, Ima and her lawyer departed.

I went back to my office, where old Wiley was waiting. He seemed perplexed at the smile on my face. He was doubly confused when I said to him, "Wait around; in about a half-hour, we'll get a phone call." "What are you talking about?" he asked. I told him that I strongly suspected that in about a half-hour to an hour -- the time it would take Ima's lawyer to return to his office -- I would get a call, wherein, essentially, the lawyer would accept my previous offer of a $2,000 settlement. Wiley looked up at me in awe, awaiting some sort of explanation. How had this magic, this seemingly miracle blast out of the quicksand pit, come about? Since it had not yet happened, I felt constrained to withhold an explanation.

As though preordained, about 45 minutes later my phone rang. With the confidence and conceit of destiny, I had no doubt that it was the call I had predicted and was awaiting. It was. Ima's lawyer said, "I don't know what possessed my client, but for some reason she insists that I accept your previous offer. I'm sure I could do better at trial, but she says she simply wants to get the matter over with. So if you will draw up the papers, we can conclude this matter. None of them looked like any prize to me." I did not edify counsel.

I did, however, tell the good news immediately to Wiley. I explained my ruse de guerre. "But," he asked, "how were you so sure that she would take the bait?" As I indicated, if a person carries a "stigma" of guilt for such a long period of time, there is no one who can extract that knowledge without the person's conscious willingness. A psychologist might readily suspect or surmise the hangup, but it would be only a theory. All of us have at least one inner secret that we will never divulge. I believed that I had found the lock for which Ima had thrown away the key. She did not even tell her attorney, who, had he known, would have scoffed at the irrelevance of this meaningless data.

Exuberant and self-congratulatory in victory, it was a number of days before I looked at my conduct in a different light. In the aftermath of euphoria, I had to judge myself. Had I gone alone beyond my role as attorney? Had I played God, or his creature, Mr. Shyster? Had indeed the end justified the means? What license did I have to turn the screws on someone, regardless of her character, morality, or even purpose, who was engaged in a dispute that had nothing whatsoever to do with the legal paternity of her genes?

I honestly felt that I had done something that may not have met high professional standards, and while I do not believe I have done anything quite like it since, I cannot say with conviction that I would not do similarly in the same type of situation. The dichotomy of the standards is unavoidable.

Lawyers are, and are supposed to be, human. It is true that nurse Ima was not really a caricature of Nurse Ratched in "Cuckoo's Nest," any more than Wiley was Bob Cratchit in

"Christmas Carol." Still, the weighing of right and wrong in this case was too pronounced to be ignored.

What I had done was neither illegal nor immoral. It was probably not unethical. But was it right? I simply do not know and do not think there is an unqualified answer. Each case must be pondered individually. Certain things are, however, clear. First, and in this instance probably foremost, my client was "saved." Secondly, attorneys will consciously, or otherwise, do those -- legal -- things that are necessary to bring about the desired result. Whatever they should be, lawyers should not be potted plants. Finally, from my point of view, with the admitted human limitations of visibility, the result avoided an injustice; and justice must be to the law what health is to medicine.

* * * * *

> "...A man who hungers and thirsts after justice is not satisfied with a menu. It is not enough for him to hope or believe or know that there is absolute justice in the universe; he must taste and see it. It is not enough that there may be justice some day in the golden haze of the future; it must be now; it must <u>always</u> have been now. "The Book of Job", Stephen Mitchell, <u>Tikkun</u>, Vol. 1, p. 56, 63 (1986)

But, in the end, each of us must draw the line where he will, where his innards and conscience lead him. All of us must have some point of insistence or resistance. I do not think I went beyond that point of what a lawyer should or should not do. To allow an injustice is no less than to cause it. As Man Ray stated many years ago, "Each of us, in his own timidity, has limits beyond which he is outraged." I was to learn in the years to come that the limits of some of us, lawyers included, are so unexplored that they do not exist.

Chapter 4.

Lawyers in the Dock (Part I):
The Rise and Decline of a Noble Profession

Since ancient times, lawyering has been one of the most criticized occupations in Western society. This is understandable. Unlike farming, soldiering, doctoring, preaching, horse-stealing and other singularly important trades or professions, lawyering deals with the full panoply of human problems in a civilized society. Time and advice, as Lincoln wrote, may be the lawyer's "stock in trade," but people, mores and power constitute his practice and purpose. Lawyering undertakes, under the color of right, to preserve and protect civilization, maintain the dominance of the state and accommodate the forever changing prerogatives, duties and mores of its inhabitants. All in the name of justice.

From, the outset, it can be argued, lawyering, even with such an expansive role, need not be based upon or even aspire to such a lofty concept as justice. An agent for a force -- and a fee -- is not a plenipotentiary; his agency does not necessarily encompass justice; he is a lobbyist for a more selfish cause. He may be an officer of the court and a gentleman to his colleagues, but, as is often contended, he is ambassadorial, adverse to claims contrary to those of his client. His writ is narrow and one-dimensional -- to serve his client. He may cede only minor ground to his opponents, and then solely to gain the greater advantage. Adherents of this school of thought would maintain that justice need not be a lawyer's badge; indeed, it may not even have to be his mask.

But, lawyering to gain a secure position in society must, by dint of effort, not only appear to serve justice but, in reality, is compelled to produce more than a modicum of that still-prized commodity. Such effort often seems opposite to the lawyer's certificate of safe passage, the limitation of his authority, the specificity of his mission. Paradoxically, however, if he fails to carry this dual duty on both shoulders, the respect (and therefore, in measure, the clout) of lawyering is bound to continue to diminish. In the wake of that inevitably comes an increased bureaucratic interpretation of law and justice, propped up by a colorable "rule of law," but bridled by a rein of arbitrary authoritarianism -- despite written "guarantees" to the contrary. Justice, to the extent it may then exist, will, to paraphrase Milan Kundera, be "justice by mistake." Such is essentially the nature of lawyering throughout the former Soviet Union, modern China, and in all totalitarian societies, whatever their democratic guise.

American lawyers have more than an academic or even a financial interest in preventing such a dismal state of affairs. The practice of law in this country, while currently witnessing withering criticism and waning favor, still retains considerable respect in the community and its practitioners remain among the elite in prestige and influence, despite public opinion polls.[4]

---

[4] A significant factor ameliorating the drop in prestige of the
(continued...)

Remove the professional (and biblical) command to seek justice and the myth of professionalism itself disappears. The lawyer becomes just another tradesman, a wordsman. For this reason alone, the lawyer must selfishly strive to reconcile the irreconcilable, the incongruous duality and the charivari band nature of his undertaking.

Carrying such an onus is scarcely altruistic. The lawyer has much to gain on a personal and psychological level -- despite the revolutionary change in values that seems to have occurred in recent times. Conversely, he loses a great deal by falling from grace. Most lawyers are ego-propelled, and nothing deflates an ego more than uselessness, whatever the endeavor. As Plato defined happiness: the opportunity to do that which man is best able to do and his being given the broadest breadth for doing it. Remove the salient search for justice from that quest and lawyering is largely drone's work.

This paradox of lawyering is hardly remarkable; paradox is often the nature of things. Something more makes lawyering Promethean. Three abiding factors make this unique role of dual citizenship, split personality and inherent conflict especially treacherous. First, the assignment of lawyering, as society has designed it, is as weighty in aspiration as it is presumptuous. Objectively, the countervailing forces lawyering seeks to rein are

---

[4](...continued)
        legal profession is that all institutions and professions have in recent years fallen in public respect. Society's moorings are being cut rapidly and the storm affects all. There is no safe haven. Still, by 1986 lawyers probably reached an historical nadir in prestige. As reported from the ABA convention that year, a poll had shown that nine out of ten people did not think the practice of law was a worthy goal for their children. Self-aggrandizement, the general public increasingly believes, is the hallmark of all those who wear the silk. Maybe that is why these same parents send their offspring to law schools in droves.

too disparate and passionate to produce anything more than, at best, a fleeting acquiescence. The search for the Golden Fleece is always shadowed by disillusion. At most, society's contending forces can be held in check and only a modicum of justice can be attained at any given time; and even then it can be retained but precariously.

Secondly, lawyers are subjectively limited in this travail. They are restricted not only by the "rules of law," but by their own normal vices. Too frequently they seem even less inhibited by the "rules" than others, thus undermining their own acceptability. Wayward preachers win few followers. Today the plethora of vices of those in the profession is expanding so alarmingly that the claim that lawyering is still a profession is at least open to honest debate. The modern law firm surely is, as never before, more a business -- with all its inherent competitive pitfalls -- than it is engaging in an art or science.

The foregoing observations are fairly apparent. A third consideration -- aggravating the dilemma-- is, however, less clear and more controversial. In the end, this factor may be more overriding than all others in weighing the value of lawyering -- at least the moral value.

Law and justice. They are not the same and few make such a contention. Generally the courts, to their credit, do not. But law and justice need not be made incompatible; and lawyers, to qualify as professionals, have a mandate to make them as palatable to each other as humanly possible. Justice, without or in derogation of the law, undermines a civilized order. Conversely, the application of the law so as to work a travesty or even to ignore a just end is a disguised crime. To these proper values all concerned have an immediate duty. And the lawyer's is the greater. Indifference will not avoid the sometimes clear but always present predicament. The chalice of being society's emissaries for justice has been handed to lawyers, not as a gift, but as a responsibility.

The judicial system can serve the state only as long as it serves the individual. Unlike all the totalitarian systems, our organized society is not bottomed on its own preservation foremost; the individual and individual justice is our escutcheon. This is not a universal or even a Western truth; but it is ours, or at least mine. The law, in all its pronounced majesty, is but a handmaiden to that individual justice. The power of that single concept -- too often overlooked -- must always permeate.

Indeed, the Talmud, the fount of the unending search for justice through law, is unyielding in its insistence that the latter is but the servant of the former. As potent a force as is the adherence to law in Judaic thought, its misuse at the expense of justice is probably as great a sin as there can be.[5] Thus, a rabbi may be forgiven for virtually any transgression -- no matter how base. Only one sin is unforgivable. If a rabbi uses the law in a literal way that was hardly intended, and that interpretation causes an individual an injustice, the rabbi is to be shunned. The sanctity of the law cannot be a vehicle for bringing about an unjust result. That is the highest principle. A lawyer must never lose sight of that lodestar.

* * * * *

The late, renowned Oxford law professor, H.L.A. Hart, a leading advocate of the so-called "Positivist" school of jurisprudence, probably would have differed strongly with what I have just referred to as the "highest principle." He (and Jeremy Bentham and John Austin, well over a century before him) would have likely criticized this "natural law" concept of legality. Hart

---

[5] At other times the commentators indicate that the greatest sin a man can commit is to fail to teach his child a trade. Interestingly, whether this or the perversion of the law is of greater importance, both in the end deal with the rights of individuals, not society or even God.

had insisted that there was and should remain a distinction between "what is" and "what ought to be." He urged that law and justice need not necessarily be made compatible, let alone the same.

In a stout and scholarly defense of his stance, in 1957 Hart delivered the famous annual Holmes Lecture at Harvard Law School. In it (and in a subsequent written version), he raised the thorny problem of law in derogation of justice in the context of an enthralling case that arose in West Germany some time after World War II. That classic case bears powerful witness that this issue or principle is more than an "innocent pastime for philosophers." Ironically, the paramountcy of moral law was poignantly underscored by a German court in 1949 in an ultimate defiance of the legal foundation of Nazism.

The stern facts of this eerie case are as follows: The defendant, in 1944, desiring to rid herself of her husband (reputedly for another man), reported to the authorities various derogatory remarks the husband had made about Hitler while home on leave from the German Army, knowing well the consequences of her action. She thereafter testified against him before a military court, and the husband was sentenced to death by that tribunal pursuant to statutes making it illegal either to assert or repeat statements undermining the Third Reich. The death sentence was never carried out; instead, he was imprisoned and then sent to the Russian front, where the survival rate for non-commissioned officers was extremely low.

Following the defeat of the Nazi regime, the wife was indicted under an old German criminal code provision for the unlawful deprivation of another's liberty. Notwithstanding the provisions of the applicable law at the time, which seemed to create a duty that she report her husband's insulting statements, the German court found that the wife was guilty. Though she acted pursuant to existing statutory law (at a time when such conduct was strongly encouraged), her actions, the court said, were "contrary to the sound conscience and sense of justice of all decent human beings." According to German law, her motive should not have been relevant in establishing the legality of the act, but in this instance that rule of law was overlooked.

Hart, while sympathetic to the court's objective in that case, dissented from the verdict. Justice -- the punishing of a woman for an "outrageously immoral act" -- cannot properly be achieved at the expense of the sanctity of the law itself, he argued. If punishment must be meted out, he asserted, it should have been done by enacting a retrospective law specifically to apply to this case. This bill-of-attainder type of justice, he maintained, odious as it might be, "would at least have the merits of candor."

Most authorities who have probed this dilemma apparently differ with Hart. The bill-of-attainder solution may be anathema to the very concept of justice, even assuming its (dubious) legality. At any rate, such a "solution" is hardly feasible. While such a device might be resorted to in a few notorious instances, the multitude of these legal predicaments (though seldom so glaring) makes special legislation to handle them totally impractical. Furthermore, during the Nazi regime (as the <u>Harvard Law Review</u> noted in discussing this case in 1950), in order to support the then existing German public law, which was both arbitrary and devoid of morality, officials disseminated and had to rely upon such popular, positivist slogans as "<u>Gesetz ist Gesetz</u>" (law is law). It is exquisitely appropriate that a post-war <u>German</u> court should resort to Talmudic teachings to denounce Hitler's law.

These moral dilemmas are not simply esoteric exercises left to the legal philosophers. In more mundane forms, to be sure, lawyers frequently encounter (but often skirt) these sensitive situations in their practices. Many claims and controversies of clients raise the conflict between law and justice, though the facts may only subtly reveal the conundrums. The nettlesome problems remain, nonetheless, though the lawyer may not focus on them -- when he winks, turns a blind eye, or fails even to perceive the quandary.

* * * * *

This principle I speak of is, of course, as difficult as it is important to pursue. Immediately, a dichotomy will be declared. We are not gods, many lawyers will argue. Ours is not to decide when we shall or shall not apply the law, to determine whether that law is good or bad. We take it as it is and simply do the best we can with it on our clients' behalf.

This comfortable defense, not without honest and highly respected adherents, is but a defense for the comfortable. It is generally a copout, an escape from the discomfort, drudgery, time and effort that justice frequently requires; it can become a license to evil. Its raison d'etre was shattered at Nuremberg. Its school is often attended by skilled attorneys, experts in the art of "papering" opponents to death or manipulating court calendars to gain undue advantage. Resorting to clever chicanery has become the pride of the competent as much as it is both the bane and the goal of the less competent lawyer. Fostering frivolous lawsuits or claims for the legal blackmail that is often available; or even threatening same, which is often as effective. Smelling out "deep-pockets" or simply advising a client not to pay a bona fide debt on the proposition that the creditor will be forced to come to terms. The innumerable slick techniques would exhaust the imagination of Torquemada. And quite often these machinations accomplish exactly the result that clients seek, and without clearly transgressing the literal letter of the "acceptable" rules.

But a higher calling commands -- as in the Hippocratic dictate, the first commandment -- that the harm not be spread. Lawyers should supply balm, not just bullets.

This duality of duty is even inherent in the Canon of Ethics; and from time to time the emphasis shifts as to the final, final duty. The conflict can never end, of course. The borderline is fuzzy. But the direction and emphasis is critical, and there are faint inklings that are encouraging. Amidst the pronounced diminution of ethics in the profession, the movement towards the greater principle is perceptively, if only peripherally, inching favorably. It manifests itself in such an unheralded requirement (now increasingly enforced in the practice more than in the breach) that attorneys bring to the attention of the court any authority on matters in contention that undermine, not simply uphold, that attorney's legal position.

Even more significant, and therefore more controversial, is the imposition of sanctions against an attorney who fails to prevent his client from perpetuating a crime or who permits the commission of what the attorney perceives may be perjury. The scope of the extension of duty in these situations is still unclear; that it is broad and important is nonetheless patent. That "winning" and "protecting the client" are but secondary goals is a proposition that is now more than a shibboleth, being championed even in Gilead, even by some of the envious, even in these "I am entitled" times. That in itself is of singular encouragement, a harbinger of hope.

It is probably, however, a losing Sysiphean effort. Given what appears to be a universal loosening of moral moorings; the undermining of institutions; the loss of community; the lack of respect for the rule of law; the total victory of the force of "rights" against the beleaguered advocates of "duty" (the first four-letter word); the absence of effective peer and judicial review; how can one have any confidence whatsoever that lawyering will defy and rise above its surroundings? Optimism in the face of this reality is folly.

A very succinct historical focus is in order: Lawyering, like Western society itself, has become subservient to the dominant estate that has emerged in the past 200 years -- the so-called populace. Popular will, of course, needs restraints, and lawyers were vested with the role of helping to create, execute, and most importantly, interpret the wise restraints that make men free.

Because of its importance to all the estates, but particularly the Third Estate, lawyering soon became the dominant profession, scorned on repeated occasions but generally, if grudgingly, admired. The lawyer, almost to the extent of the landowner, exercises authority in the absence of more powerful historical institutions that usually held sway in Europe. Men's lives and liberties, in the United States in particular, seem to be determined in the courts. As de Tocqueville noted with astonishment 150 years ago, almost all of society's problems, even those political in nature, came to wend their way to the bench. Lawyering, rather than the political process itself, was perhaps the principal means of permitting the <u>vox populi</u> to become articulate and effective.

Americans, as de Tocqueville further observed, may be a litigious people. They are probably so, however, in a more formal manner and only because the roads to the court are not impaired; and a democracy without a history of authoritarian institutions must find its authoritative forum somewhere. The courts serve as our Roman Forum, Coliseum, and Tabernacle. Our diversity limits class. Our history militates against the military. Our constitution confines the religious reach to its non-secular domain. The courthouse is our charterhouse.

From the inception of the country, as Lord Bryce emphasized a hundred years ago, "There were no reactionary conspirators to be feared, for everyone prized liberty and equality. There were no questions between classes, no animosities against rank and wealth, for rank and wealth did not exist." Our courts are now not only the ultimate but often the initial forums for our business and entrepreneurial decisions. They have even become the arbitrators for our religious feuds and the umpires for our military excursions. Their jurisdiction is unfenced.

Today, courts and their instruments -- lawyers -- deal with problems that even their recent predecessors in the profession scarcely envisioned. Can, for instance, a president legally conduct a foreign policy in one manner rather than another? May a man sleep with one or two women or other men with impunity? Must a woman, as a matter of law, be paid for her pregnancy? Is it proper that a child be born from the womb of someone other than his "mother" and from the sperm of someone other than his "father," and what are the rights of all five? Is it a violation of fundamental rights to have a 25-hour day? May a child sue his parents for not being good parents? Is wearing a yarmulke rightfully forbidden by military law though commanded by a higher law? Can a state fire a policeman primarily because he is over 40? Or white? What is a family? Can an employee squeal on his boss, and must the boss then continue to employ him? Promote him? Must a terminal, comatose patient be force-fed, with or without his permission? These and endless other questions are the fodder (and the bounty) of many practicing lawyers. The law is no longer essentially dowagers' rights, the Rule in Shelley's Case, the sale of Blackacre, or the like. Modern society has not solved these recurring problems. It has merely gone far beyond them.

In light of the unbounded scope of lawyering, there is the serious question as to whether the practice of law is professionally possible. Certainly, the average attorney or judge is not knowledgeable enough to deal with such immense and multitudinous questions of complexity. We can scorn the absence of simplicity, but all the bellowing against complexity will not produce simple, let alone correct, answers. Professionalism is primarily an "approach." Most lawyers find it necessary to specialize to be professional in anything more than "approach." The complexity and quantity of litigation, unfortunately, encourage the opportunists. Thus, whereas in former years professionalism itself was an ideal to be pursued, protected, and handled with care and pride, today, under the camouflage of complexity and under the pressure of caseloads, many lawyers too often manipulate a result in defiance of professional aims; courts, overwhelmed, can scarcely control the flotsam. The adversary system, the bulwark of Anglo-Saxon law, exacerbates the predicament. Despite much merit in this process as a method for ferreting out the truth, too often it is a lawyer's license for legal licentiousness.

Surely, previous generations of attorneys have noted with some likely correctness the waning of professional standards, and there has never been, obviously, a generation of lawyers that has not had its scoundrels, dolts and misfits and a plenitude of judges who serve nothing but their own egos. It took generations of accumulation to require the Herculean effort necessary to make the Augean stables habitable. Still, in the past few years alone any court-watcher would have had to have been out to lunch to fail to note, in an almost direct proportion to the increase in the number of lawyers, a decrease in professional lawyering.

I suspect that in the final analysis, given the impossible role of lawyering in a society that demands swift and simple answers but professes that they be fair, there is no solution to this state of affairs. It is how we deal with the problem that is important. Are lawyers able to be professional, or are they merely granted charters by the community to be fundraisers for themselves? Are they now nothing more than members of the bourgeoisie, drawing dividends from a semi-mythical glorious past? No longer can it be said, as de Tocqueville did, that the bar is where "the American aristocracy is found." Winning cases is too often the sole mark of accomplishment and success. In our present society, that is understandable. From a professional point of view, we must <u>insist</u>: <u>quo</u> <u>warranto</u>?

Chapter 5.

From Out of the West . . . The Lone Wranglers

When I started practicing law at the end of the Fifties, and for a number of years thereafter, whatever success I enjoyed was primarily as an outgrowth of labor and luck. By prevailing in most of my cases, moreover, I was able to achieve favorable settlements in additional matters that would otherwise not have been attainable. Still, neither the general public nor the bulk of the legal community had the slightest notion of who I was or what I was doing in the practice of law; for all practical purposes, the knowledge of my successes was confined to a coterie of clients, associates and informed judges. I had won cases involving millions of dollars, some dealing with major issues, still others affecting the immediate lives of many people in the most significant ways. My premature obituary, however, pretty much would have been limited to time and place. My relative anonymity in the larger community is typical of most attorneys, especially younger ones.

Then one day in the mid-Sixties, a matter of the most ordinary kind came my way. I received this case solely because, in the course of pursuing my specialty, labor law, I had gained considerable experience (and some limited professional notice) with injunctive proceedings. This new matter required a twist of sorts from the typical injunctive action. An imaginative gentleman, Mr. Stay, in the early Sixties had found a new way to make a living, confounding law enforcement officials and costing supermarkets dearly.

Taking a page out of American Western history, Stay would go around various Los Angeles neighborhoods, gather and put on his truck all unchained shopping carts that supermarket customers had left about -- on the streets, lawns, backyards, wherever, but usually within a mile or two of their home market.

These carts cost a good deal more than is generally realized, then anywhere from $40 to $100 apiece. Daily, like clockwork and the Good Shepherd, Stay would steer these stray carts into his backyard corral; then, nightly, call up the individual markets, tell them that he had "found" X number of their carts and that he would bring them home -- for a monetary reward. As I recall, his asking price was about $5 each. An average daily haul might bring in 20 to 30 strays for Stay. In California and elsewhere, a code of nineteenth-century vintage permits finders of "lost" articles to claim a reward from their owners. Stay had found for himself a profitable variation of an ancient, if dubious, trade. The horse came before the cart. At any rate, even though "branded," these ambulatory bins were held openly for ransom.

The various supermarket chains sought legal help. They first went to one of the blue-ribbon law firms in Los Angeles, which advised them that they had no case. The firm opined that an injunction could not be secured because you could not enjoin a crime, assuming that what Stay was doing (taking and holding property without permission) was a crime. Given this negative advice, one market chain, in desperation, tracked me down and retained me.

When I brought the matter to court, I took a totally different tack; I argued that Stay's actions, perhaps shady, though done in the light of day, were nonetheless <u>not</u> criminal. He was, I said, engaged in a perfectly for-profit, free-enterprise venture. Far from attacking Stay, I flattered him. Indeed he was, I stated, covering tongs with cheek, a good Samaritan.[6]

Such was not a crime, I urged upon the court; rather, it was but an inadvertent civil wrong and therefore could be enjoined. The carts were not "lost" and therefore were not "found" by Stay, just as in the situation where an old man has his eyeglasses on top of his head and walks around at some length searching for them. Surely, the spectacles were not lost; the old man would eventually locate them. So, too, markets, with ordinary diligence and in reasonably short order, would locate the carts in neighboring stores, alleys, parking lots and alongside freeways.

The judge bought this analogy, holding that the carts were not lost, merely misguided. He issued an injunction preventing Stay from seeking a reward for any cart within a one-mile radius of the market in question. This court-made rule, interestingly enough, remained for many years the metes and bounds of impermissible rustling. With that ruling, Stay had conducted his last roundup.

---

[6] My "candor" harks back to this possibly apocryphal story: Some years ago, a lawyer, arguing a case before the United States Supreme Court, was asked by Justice Brandeis if it were not true that if the Court failed to accept one of the lawyer's important rationales, then the lawyer's entire case, like a house of cards, would fall to pieces. The lawyer unflinchingly replied that such a result would logically be required. Justice Brandeis, appreciative of this unusual forthrightness, thanked the attorney for his "candidness." Just then the buzzer on the lectern sounded, indicating that the Court was to recess for lunch before resuming oral argument. The justices duly filed singly by the counsel table on their way out of the courtroom. As Justice Holmes walked past the "honest" lawyer, he leaned over and (knowing his Tartuffe) whispered to that counsel, "Candidness, sir, is the subtlest form of deception there is."

At least within the proscribed geographical area, he found himself out of business.

The case, despite its somewhat whimsical nature and immediate consequence to the litigants, would not seem to have been of major import to the future of jurisprudence. Indeed, I might well have forgotten the case except that a funny thing happened on the way out of the forum that made the case indelible, at least to me. And it was not much more than an offhand remark that turned this case into one of personal significance.

At the close of the oral argument, in summing up, in an impromptu phrase I urged the court to enjoin the "cartnapping." The term apparently never had been used before and, fortuitously, a local newspaper reporter in the courtroom seized an "angle" and ran a feature story on the case the next morning, highlighting the newly coined term. In turn, the wire services picked up the line and carried it from coast to coast. From that one little waggish remark I received more publicity in the community, nationwide and professionally than I had from the dozens of cases I had handled successfully up to that time; for weeks, clients and others called or wrote me to comment upon "cartnapping." I immediately enjoyed the reaction; but then I wondered about it. I soon became concerned about, and later resigned to, the implications of this kind of experience.

* * * * *

Actually, the "message" should hardly have come as a surprise. A few years earlier, while a third-year law student, I was a firsthand witness to the -- often near impudent -- ways and wiles by which lawyers would promote and parlay publicity to gain profits (or power). Forty years ago, San Francisco's Melvin Belli, the self-styled "King of Torts," was at the height of his successful career. His flair for the dramatic, both in and outside the courtroom, coupled with a keen legal skill, had brought him national recognition and clientele. His antics, however, often were, in their outlandishness, somewhat ahead of his time. So, occasionally, was the subtlety of his tactics.

Law reviews, then as now, were usually the intellectual citadels of legal society (despite the fact that Justice Holmes once referred to them as "the work of boys"). Being published by the leading law reviews carried with it considerable prestige. Belli undoubtedly recognized that this "showman" approach to his particular practice needed to be supplemented by the appearance of scholarship. The <u>Yale Law Journal</u> would make a very good vehicle to this end, he apparently concluded.

One morning, in the garret offices of the <u>Journal</u> in New Haven, we received a telegram from the Western boondocks -- California. From the famous Melvin Belli. In it, he announced that he was wiring this telegram to us while the jury was deliberating a verdict in one of his important products liability cases. He was, he went on to inform us, also completing a "major" and "important" article on that subject that would have a profound influence upon the development of the law and would impress appellate court judges. He would give the <u>Journal</u> the privilege of publishing this significant contribution to the law. "Please wire back immediately."

We (Easterners) reacted to this offer in a most predictable manner. Insulted that he was attempting to pull the woolsack over our eyes, offended that he sought to compromise the objectivity of our austere publication, and indignant that he, in such a blatantly self-serving fashion, was trying to treat us as bumpkins, we gave him frosty Yankee justice (vengeance): we ignored him.

It was just a few months later, coincidentally, while still on the <u>Journal</u> staff, that I experienced another encounter with a famous personage who would display a similar effrontery to our professional pride. Senator Estes Kefauver of Tennessee -- another Western wrangler -- had in 1952, and again in 1956, run for President wearing a coon-skin cap and using as his theme song "Davy Crockett" -- almost taking the nomination by storm. Despite outward appearances, he was no hayseed, however. An intelligent attorney and politician (indeed, a graduate of Yale Law School), he had a once-deserved reputation for being quite knowledgeable in the area of antitrust law.

In 1958, still harboring another run for the Presidency (against John F. Kennedy, who in 1956 he had beat out for the Vice Presidential nomination), Senator Kefauver spoke at Yale Law School. He took this occasion to visit the Journal staff. He, too, recognized that he had to alter his image; a scholarly facade would suit him better in a statesman-like presidential campaign than his now discarded coon skin.

"Boys," he said to us, "how would you like to publish an article I'm thinking of writing on the antitrust problem?" We gathered around him more closely. Naturally, we were interested. But we held our professional reserve. "What is it specifically you had in mind, Senator?," we asked. And we started to probe. Sipping his cocktail and ogling the female students milling around, the 55-year-old graduate soon made it clear that he didn't have much on his mind relating to antitrust. In fact, he didn't have a single idea or theme relating to any article on the subject. His mind clearly was not focused on corporate hanky-panky.

He had obviously made his offer on the spur of the moment, though no doubt aware than an article of his in a scholarly law review would partially offset a potential rival's prize-winning book entitled Profiles of Courage. Resentful that we were being used and collectively concluding that any article he might send to us would be vacuous, we were careful not to urge him to submit anything to us; for if we "invited" a manuscript, we would almost be bound to publish it. Instinctively, we deftly changed the subject. The Senator went off to other things.

Later, I was to learn that it is fairly easy for "boys" to put down or turn away from would-be kings and two-time presidential candidates; but to turn down paying clients, ah, that's another story.

Chapter 6.

Lawyers in the Dock (Part II): Raiders of the Lost Art

In the decades since 1958, the practice of law has changed immensely in a variety of ways. Not only have the courts increasingly become the arena for deciding political and social questions, but they are now also the battleground for assertive rights that formerly had been the bailiwick of the legislature or had evolved and were in the domain of the streets. Most Americans now seemingly believe, even more than de Tocqueville discerned in 1840, that all important questions would eventually be in the realm of, and resolved by, the courts. This was made manifest by the astonishing attention given by the American people since 1987 to the confirmation hearings of would-be Supreme Court justices.

The social and political history of the United States, as discussed previously, ushered in the primary role of the judiciary. Other factors assured its continued paramount position: the myth and aura of its objectivity, the willingness of the other branches of government to accede to this power; the belief that this was the least dangerous branch; finally, <u>faut</u> <u>de</u> <u>mieux</u> -- there is no alternative to having the democratic experiment work. Many of today's problems, however, turn on the fact that this aura and myth have patently begun to wane, to be weakened in a serious manner.

The rule of law -- the sanctity of the courts -- at the threshold of the Twenty-First Century can no longer be taken for granted. The precarious nature of the very existence of an ordered society receives no headlines. This critical plight has no Sputniks to shock us into action. It has no October stock market crashes to bring us to our senses. It is a slow, disquieting strangulation.

The courts, moreover, are in the unenviable position that this tenuous, or growing lack of, respect for the rule of law results in a beleaguered judiciary unable to counterattack. The courts, Canute-like, cannot recreate the social and political environment that permitted the rule of law, as interpreted by the courts, to reign supreme. Though most courts fight valiantly, and with limited success, the tide keeps rolling in. In 1942, Judge Learned Hand, in addressing himself to the fundamental principles of equity and fair play, wrote that:

> "...a society so riven that the spirit of moderation is gone, no court <u>can</u> save; that a society where that spirit flourishes, no court <u>need</u> save; that in a society which evades its responsibility by thrusting upon the courts the nurture of that spirit, that spirit in the end will perish."

It is ironic that, in this uneasy milieu, lawyers have become ever more visible and vulnerable. In the explosion of the law's process, not only have they become more prone to attack and be attacked, but they are also more invested in their clients' causes, gains and losses. They have become frontiersmen in a legal free-for-all. Coupled with the fact that lawyering is done mainly in the impersonal urban centers, where there is greater opportunity for material and status success, this involvement invites adulteration of professional standards.

The growth of the lawyering industry -- given the complexity of society and the nature of the social and political mores and institutions of the country -- was inevitable and is probably inexorable. Still, the growth has probably extended beyond a realistic demand or need. During the past fifty years, the percentage of lawyers in relation to the population has doubled. In California, which is merely ahead of, rather than simply different from, the rest of the country, lawyering is one of the state's largest expanding industries. Indeed, the day is almost inevitable when law firms will (with some appropriate restrictions) be bought and sold on the stock market.

The number of lawyers in California has expanded to almost 150,000, over six times the number of lawyers that existed in the state three decades before, even though the population has risen only from 17 million to 32 million. In that span of time almost one out of every hundred new residents (men, women and children) is a lawyer.

Nationwide, the barodynamic statistics are almost as startling: the number of attorneys in the past 25 years has more than doubled. That this "plague" of lawyers is not confined to the megalopolis centers of the country but has even spread across the prairies is seen by the fact that in Iowa (of all places) during the Eighties the population had fallen about three percent, but the number of lawyers has skyrocketed 22 percent. There are nationwide, in addition, presently approximately 125,000 law students annually who will join these privileged ranks.

But the deluge of lawyers appears to have aggravated, rather than alleviated, the problem confronted by society and the courts -- and the aims of the profession. At times, it seems that progress is as much blocked by the more skilled and intelligent lawyers as by their less competent colleagues. The apparent surplus of lawyers is actually fostering litigation, promoting publicity gimmicks, and reducing the efficacy of peer watchdogging. Even more -- contrary to the expectation of many -- it has helped to propel lawyers' fees out of the reach of most Americans, and it has encouraged lawyers to become shills in the marketplace.

In order to survive and/or achieve success, many attorneys tout themselves in ways unheard of and usually prohibited in times past. Necessity has a way of winning out, and publicity-prone attorneys have, for the most part, been given the green light to engage in such practices. The yuppie lawyer is often first and foremost a publicist.

Years ago, most attorneys and certainly the established bar frowned upon lawyers engaging in even the slightest bit of advertising or solicitation. The bar looked with disfavor, to say the least, upon those members who sought to have their names -- or even allowed their names -- in the newspapers. Like those families in the reigning and original Blue Book, their names were to be in the public press only at the time of their birth, their marriage, and their death. The publicity that the "cartnapping" incident produced would have been suspect a few generations ago, and the bar would have looked askance upon a lawyer who permitted such discussion of his case in the press.

A residue of that former professional standard, which even then could be criticized as too rigid, may still exist. Often, these professional restrictions were petty. I recall, for example, that a lawyer friend of mine was officially admonished by the bar for sending Christmas cards to his clients that pictured his staff, including the office cleaning woman with her mop and pail! This was only twenty-five years ago. But given the onrushing changes in society and the courts' letting down the barriers, both in advertising and in opening court proceedings to the electronic media, the attorney who fights his cases outside the courtroom or uses the court as a stage is becoming the norm. It is as inevitable as it is regrettable.

Most lawyers today will go to unprecedented lengths to capture not only their present and potential clients' fancies, but also the general public's attention. Lawyers have become only secondarily "officers of the court." In becoming full-blown participants in, and real parties-in-interest to, their clients' causes, what dignity lawyers did have has been compromised. Increased competition and the greater impersonality of society will continue to insure this result. Lawyers, like other professionals, have openly and uncompromisingly joined the free enterprise system. They hawk their services without compunction; they peg their fees to whatever the market will bear.

Indeed, one of the most notable depictions of the degree to which lawyers in recent years have tended to exploit the opportunities and vulnerabilities of the marketplace is their fee structure. Mega-merger attorneys certainly have captured the public's attention in this regard as have the multitudes of products liability cases. Lawyers in the family law specialty, as an example, often deliberately entwine their clients' fortunes with their own. Thus, on the trendy West Side of Los Angeles, some attorneys publicly and piously urge their colleagues to demonstrate a "willingness" to serve the community in this very sensitive field of law because it deals with "families in crisis." At the same time, many of these "specialists" shamelessly have established fee formulas that should shock the conscience of the unwary. Not only do they now charge as much as $300 or more per hour to achieve "justice" for one of the family members in crisis, but the lawyers will, incidentally, reap a bountiful harvest. One fashionable fee contract that has made the rounds states, that in addition to the guaranteed hourly fee just noted:

> "The total fee for our services will be determined at the time of our final billing to you. The fee will depend upon the difficulties encountered, the complexity of the litigation, and the results achieved on your behalf. If at that time we, within our discretion, believe that we have received more in fees than what we believe to be a reasonable

fee, we will refund the excess to you. But the final billing will not be less than the total number of hours multiplied by the applicable hourly rates.

Translation from the legalese:

If you win, your attorney wins. If you win big, your attorney wins big. If you lose, your attorney wins. No other component of the capitalist system has such rewards with so little risk.

So brazen are many attorneys in advertising their cunningness that they appear to have no compunctions about bragging about it on the public record. For example, at an annual convention of plaintiff attorneys in New Hampshire in the summer of 1995 (in a lovely sylvanic setting), attorneys touted their techniques for going after "deep pockets." One speaker after another at this conclave spoke about how you can bring individuals and companies in as defendants though they have but a tenuous relationship to the alleged tort wrongdoing. Thus, if an individual defendant doesn't have enough money, these attorneys are alert to the fact that they can plead their complaints in such a way as to not only bring in innocent employers but also insurance companies who would "raise the kitty." Thus, one speaker said, "You can accomplish a lot through insurance law" by pleading a claim that could be covered which will trigger the duty to defend, adding that once the carrier is in and spending money on the case, it's a contributor to settlement. The ball game, so to speak. That same attorney then stated that if you make a credible demand in excess of the policy limits, and you create a situation where the carrier has unreasonably failed to settle within the policy limits, they are effectively waived, which will "up the ante" on the other side. Such conduct is not illegal. Still, it causes conniptions not only with insurance companies and opposing counsel and their clients, but with the public at large -- except of course, plaintiffs.

This <u>laissez-faire</u> mode of lawyering, in the center and setting of a service economy, has both the trappings and traps of the Wall Street scene. The "legal service industry" now employs over two million people, including lawyers, paralegals, secretaries, accountants, managers, and other support personnel and retainers. Not only are lawyers spearheading their tycoon clients' battles, they are fashioning carbon copies of these same raiding tactics within the legal community itself. Thus, in the past few years, full-scale, methodically planned raids by one law firm on the internal human assets of another law firm even down to the mailroom -- have become a recognized norm. Mergers, takeovers and buyouts -- offers that cannot be refused -- are as familiar between the law firms as they are among their clients. Like their clients on the Big Board, law firms unabashedly have begun to hire public relations companies to wrap and vent their wares. Often, even gentility is abandoned in the pirating of clients.

In the end, an M.B.A. may become a prerequisite for an LL.B. Perhaps, even vice-versa. The niceties of the art come to merge (if they do not completely yield to) the needs of the business. Lawyers may have gotten themselves into a classic double-bind: to "succeed," they are adopting the ethics of their Wall Street clients; in doing so, they are losing their raison d'etre and the respect of society.

Chapter 7.

Judges on Trial:
From Couch to Bench and Vice Versa

It is hardly a revelation to announce that judges, every bit as much as legislators, make law. Everyone who has -- or assumes -- power makes law, one way or another. Parents, to a lessening, and children to an increasing extent, make law. It is the finesse in covering up this exercise that misleads.

One outstanding former jurist recently and candidly stated the reality. The late Otto Kaus, a practicing attorney for many years, served thereafter as a California trial and appellate judge, and State Supreme Court justice. He then returned to the practice of law in 1988. In an oral interview, in defining the role of judges, he stated what some other jurist-scholars have in more pedantic terms revealed:

> "It's a lot of things. It's trying to find a solution to
> a knotty problem. First of all, you have to find out
> if somebody else has found a solution first. And

if they have, then that kind of confines you in what you can do. If nobody has and you're satisfied that this is an undiscovered territory, then you're really free to say what you think the law ought to be. If nobody says you're wrong, then you're saying what the law is. Whether a political theory says that you are not supposed to make the law, the fact is, when you're confronted with an unprecedented problem, usually to decide the case you have to make the law. There is no way out of it, that's what you get paid for.

That's letting the kitty out of the wool sack.

Judges -- lawmakers -- "make" law whether they are conservative or liberal, loose or strict constructionists, conscious of what they do or otherwise. And such terms are but labels -- talismanic aids to tell you the generic nature of that inside the jar but little about its quality or true flavor. Sometimes, admittedly, those labels allow you to predict; after all, that is in part what lawyers get paid to do -- foretell results by probing the nuances of the Court of Chance. But the best way to predict what a judge will do is not so much to listen to his avowed philosophy, but to probe his intelligence, psyche, character, club, and, at times, his penchant to admire his own penmanship.

. . . Crack in the Concrete . . .

My first and most revealing encounter with Judge Thurmond Clarke took place in 1961. While leaving my office one evening at around six o'clock, I literally had one foot in the elevator when, from another elevator, two very excited men emerged, plaintively inquiring if there were a labor attorney about. Quickly jumping back off the elevator, I advised them that I was indeed such an animal. They, in fact, were looking for me, with a tale of woe and a need for immediate succor. Earlier that day they had been served with an order signed by federal district court Judge Thurmond Clarke, enjoining their company and each of them individually from allowing the work of pouring and scoring concrete to be done by members of the Cement Masons Union, or anyone other than members of the Laborers Union. The facts were as follows:

The company was building a huge, multimillion dollar shopping center. The parking lot for the center was being finished in concrete and had to be scored within the next 24 hours or the entire concrete lot would crack, requiring it to be all dug up and poured again at tremendous cost. The type of work in question had been in dispute between the two unions for some time, but generally had been done by the Cement Masons. Judge Clarke's order precluded the Cement Masons from doing the work, despite the employer's contract with that union, and, in effect, awarded the work to the Laborers Union, which the employer felt had neither the right nor the ability to do the work. This was clearly a jurisdictional labor dispute, in which the employer had become an innocent victim. In this predicament, unless Judge Clarke's order were overturned, the employer could only be seriously damaged.

Although Clarke was generally considered to be an earnest and fair-minded judge, his limitations, at least in labor law, were striking. It was readily apparent to any lawyer, let alone one knowledgeable in labor law, that his order was patently erroneous for a variety of reasons. First of all, he had no jurisdiction (authority) under the Norris-LaGuardia Act. That statute, among other things, prohibits a federal district court from granting an injunction in any labor dispute, except with narrow and clearly defined exceptions. Moreover, he was plainly barred by the United States Supreme Court cases from taking such action that was primarily, if not solely, within the jurisdiction of the National Labor Relations Board. Furthermore, the evidence before the judge was woefully inadequate to grant any such injunction, apart from its probable dire results. Finally, he inexplicably gave the order without any notice whatsoever being given to the employer or the other union.

I worked all night, resolving to go to the judge's chambers the first thing next morning and beseech him to reverse his position and revoke the injunction. I finished preparing all the necessary papers, including mimeographing and collating them, by early morning. After leaving a telephone message for opposing counsel, I dashed seven blocks to the federal court building, literally barged into the judge's chambers and proceeded to race to his desk, from which he looked up at me, astonished. I dropped the mass of documents virtually into his lap, and then, without invitation, engaged in an uninterrupted, rapid, three-minute monologue as to why the court had inadvertently and erroneously signed the order and how absolutely necessary it was in the interest of justice that he sign the prepared revocation I had put before him.

Without saying an additional word, Judge Clarke looked at me and asked, "Where do I sign?" I eagerly showed him. He took his pen out of his pocket and put his signature to the paper with a bold flourish. Without another word, I snatched up the signed document and fled his chambers. After quickly filing the document at the clerk's office, I returned to my office and advised my client that "God's in his heaven, all's right with the world." I then telephoned, again, the attorney for the Laborers Union, Lionel Richman, who had filed the complaint. He had just arrived at his office. I had never met him, but knew he had a reputation for being imaginative.

After briefly introducing myself and telling him that I had just had the District Court sign a revocation of the injunction it had issued against my client, I said to Richman, "As a matter of curiosity, how did you ever expect any judge to sign the order you got yesterday?" He then patiently revealed to me the nature of the practice. "Well, it's like this, Mr. Tobin. My client came to me a week or so ago and told me of the Laborers' concern and desire to get this work. I told them I didn't think there was much chance, but that we had little to lose by trying." I then inquired, "But how did you expect any judge to sign it?" "I really didn't, but you see, two judges are sick, one is on vacation, and that leaves four judges sitting. I told my client that one of those judges was Thurmond Clarke. I explained my course of action to my client: I would go to the clerk's counter in the courthouse, file my complaint for an injunction, and the clerk would pick up a card and assign it to the judge on that card. There is one chance in four it will be Clarke. If it's him, then I'll go to his chambers and make my pitch as to why he should sign it. If it's one of the other three available judges, I'll immediately dismiss the complaint I just filed while I'm still standing at the clerk's counter."

I told Richman that I was astonished that he could plan such a firk, and was equally flabbergasted by his luck. "But why did you believe that Clarke would sign such an order?," I asked searchingly. "Young fellow," Richman said in rabbinic tones, "I told my client that the injunction Judge Clarke would sign would be good only until some young whippersnapper lawyer on the other side gets into court and gets him to sign a revocation." "But, why did you think that he would sign the thing in the first place and then subsequently revoke it?," I asked, still puzzled.

"Because he likes to sign his name," Richman replied. "Welcome to the practice of law, Mr. Tobin," he added, sardonically.

* * * * *

Judges, by and large, conduct themselves properly and dispense justice in the best way mortals have at their disposal. Especially on the appellate level, most judges are conscientious, hardworking and intelligent -- to a greater degree than the average attorney and far more so than the typical citizen. But they are, unfortunately, human; they will often be terribly, egregiously, even deliberately, wrong.

Indeed, a poignant illustration of such arrant judicial conduct came to my attention some 35 years after I was exposed to the foibles of Judge Clarke. And, piquantly, the same Mr. Richman was also the source of this startling, new revelation. After I sent him, in manuscript form, this collection of legal experiences, in particular this chapter relating to the episode with Judge Clarke, so that he could confirm its veracity, Richman wrote back that my "opus" was in need of a veritable "war story." Fortunately, he just happened to have one readily available:

> A bowdlerized version of the facts [he wrote] appears in the District Court of Appeal decision in <u>Annenberg v. Southern Cal. Dist. Council of Laborers</u>, [an important case the union reversed on appeal -- 38 C.A.3d 637 (1974)].
>
> Local 1184 had organized the golf course employees at the Annenberg estate and eventually took them out on strike. (The Ambassador's golf course was the largest in the desert at the time. Oh, yes, the court and counsel insisted on referring to the plaintiff as "the Ambassador.")
>
> The ambassador brought suit to enjoin all picketing. During oral argument in the makeshift Palm Springs branch of the Superior Court, [Annenberg's attorneys] argued that they did not know if any of the pickets had criminal records. (They were clean enough to work there, but of doubtful repute when they struck).
>
> I responded by advising the court that I had spent the preceding weekend reading all of the proceedings of the Select Committee on Organized Crime and could assure the court and counsel that the name of not one of the pickets appeared in that collection of volumes....which was more than I could say for the Ambassador's old man.
>
> Tumult and Confusion reigned.

The judge, who was sitting at a table across from counsel, then issued an injunction prohibiting all picketing. Since I knew Judge Metheny well from his days as Palm Springs' City Attorney, I leaned over and whispered, "Fred, this is a lot of shit." "Yes, I know," he replied, "but you don't have to run for office in this town."

* * * * *

Following the Watergate revelations in 1973-74, both the bar and the presidency were on trial. The professional dispensers of advice for the mentally concerned were having a field day. One of the nation's leading psychologists, the late Dr. Kenneth Clark, wrote and lectured that the Constitution should be amended to require that candidates for the presidency undergo psychological tests and examination. In June 1974, at a convocation on "The State of the Democratic Process," held in Beverly Hills, Dr. Clark, a former president of the American Psychological Association (exactly 12 years later he was to be awarded, by President Reagan, the nation's highest civilian award), was one of the principal speakers on a panel on "The Crisis of the Contemporary Presidency." Then-Senator Walter Mondale was on the same panel. Clark specifically called for the creation of a board of psychologists and psychiatrists to sit, as a Supreme Court of sorts, for the sole purpose of determining the fitness of all major candidates for the Presidency. (He excluded minor candidates, presumably because they were already certifiably insane.) He even suggested that the candidates, themselves, should initially be selected anonymously by their peers before running the psychological panel gauntlet. Plato's Republic revisited.

Clark's proposal, which he conceded was extreme but argued was necessary, naturally was greeted with derision by an audience composed primarily of likely patients rather than professional psychologists. "Quo custodianacis custodia?" was the instinctive and unanswerable response of the bothered but bemused audience. Mondale, perhaps prescient as to his own future, let loose a slightly nervous guffaw.

The general public and cognoscenti seem to trust psychologists even less than they trusted Nixon. Yet Clark's proposal cannot be totally ignored. Its further problem, however, is that it cannot logically begin and end with the office of the President. All officeholders should, it would seem, be subject to the same criteria. All branches of government wield tremendous power. But to apply it at all, let alone throughout the entire government apparatus, clearly is not feasible, even if it were palatable.

The consequence of the prejudices and hangups of judges are, however, as unaccountable as they are awesome. What effect upon the dispensation of justice comes from a judge's being fat and apparently liking fat ladies? How does the fact that another judge's father was a common drunkard affect the judge's sentencing? What real effect does it have on her decision in a civil rights case when a judge believes that the woman plaintiff is a lesbian? What does it mean when a judge feels that he's over his head in a complex antitrust case and that his father used to tell him he would never amount to anything. How is he affected by an attorney arguing before him who he considers to be an utter moron? Where does he displace his hostilities? How much does he care or fear he may be overruled?

The ability of a judge to cover up his mistakes or shortcomings, great as that is, is dwarfed by a judge's opportunity to have his inner purposes fulfilled with impunity, to make the appeals process merely a way of rubber-stamping the judge's aims. Few judges have both healthy <u>and</u> restrained egos. With judges having such immense power, it is hardly surprising that justice is often but a backseat driver, a mere nudge or a pesky noudge.[7]

Judges are no different from other people in regard to "getting ahead." Most judges could easily earn more money off the bench than they ever earn on it. They sacrifice -- actually claw -- to serve on courts, in large part because of the power and attendant prestige it offers. Of course, at times such vanity blinds judges and would-be judges even to themselves. In this vein, the following vignette comes to mind:

Some 40 years ago, I was the research director for Foster Furcolo, who as then running for governor in Massachusetts (successfully). I was a member of his entourage on the hustings that summer, campaigning and hustling up support and money. The latter was very hard to come by. Contributions great and small (and, one hopes, honest) were sought in every nook and cranny (read "construction company," "liquor establishment," etc.) One day a prominent attorney in the western part of the state said to the aspiring candidate, sotto voce but within my earshot, "Foster, I would like to give you a $5,000 contribution for your campaign." (At that time, this largesse was the equivalent of over $100,000 today in a California campaign.) Then came the quo pro. In the most innocent tone, he added, "I would just like one

---

[7]One disdainful practice, frequently resorted to by weak or lazy judges, is to sign whatever Findings of Facts that the prevailing attorney prepares. This makes a meaningful appeal and the appellate process a parody and an illusion. Any successful attorney worth his salty fee, who can draw up the Findings of Facts to his liking, can almost ensure that his victory is sustained on appeal. A judge who is more concerned about being upheld and adopts this "take no prisoners, kill all wounded" practice shows his unfitness for his position. That is why perceptive lawyers assert that a judge who is seldom reversed on appeal is probably an insecure judge. A strong judge will not "fix" the record to ensure his being upheld. He will give the case an impartial hearing and allow a fair appeal. He will let honest differences be focused, not interred, on appeal.

thing in return. I'd like you to appoint me to the Supreme Judicial Court. Not for me, Foster -- for Mary and the kids."!!

The infighting and manipulation of judges to gain that prestige, to be promoted, to grasp the next rung, is often only a shade more sophisticated than that same syndrome found in the business world and elsewhere. The jockeying is, if anything, often even more pretentious. Judicial vanity manifests itself in manifold ways.

An unforgettable example of this ever-present drive was indelibly impressed upon me while still a law student. I chanced to be a guest in an already packed car being driven by a distinguished district court judge from the courthouse at the end of the day. By coincidence, an equally distinguished circuit court judge emerged from the courthouse and hailed a cab. The district court judge spotted him and insisted that he be seated in the packed car and taken to his destination by the district court judge. I, being the smallest in stature by any measure, immediately found myself in a prone position on the rear seat floor.

From that unlikely vantage point, I had a worm's ear to the following discourse: A Supreme Court Justice had just passed away. A Judicial vacancy! Two openings, perhaps! No, a potential triple-play -- as many as three coveted berths to be filled! The venerable circuit court judge diplomatically suggested that he was the logical choice for the top banana post, but feared he might slip because he was not of the proper political persuasion (Ike was a Republican). The lower court judge -- of the proper persuasion -- was rightly positioned for a promotion, an opportunity toward which he was merely coy, not oblivious; the possible circuit court opening would be a cherished plum. He could, he hinted, perhaps help and be helped. So this courtly discussion went on (in judicious coda). The deal was not then consummated; but the necessary overtures had been made. It was an interesting midtown Manhattan ride, even from my lowly position.

For years, referees in bankruptcy proceedings fought tenaciously and eventually successfully to be called judges. Similarly, federal government administrative hearing officers, for generations called "trial examiners," lobbied endlessly and successfully to have their titles changed to Administrative Law Judges. In California, municipal court judges (until they reach the Superior Court) have fought continually for decades to have the municipal and superior courts merged so that they could be considered other than the lowest rank of trial judges.

Federal District Court judges almost invariably let it be known that they are "available" for a higher appointment. And in modern times, but for one recorded exception, it is unprecedented for a district judge openly to refuse a promotion. The one known exception occurred some 20 years ago when the very capable Judge Charles Wyzanski, who had served on the District Court in Boston for some 30 years (eventually to be 45 years), formally rejected a long-deserved appointment to the Circuit Court of Appeals. In explaining his rejection of that highly prized position, Judge Wyzanski poignantly noted that a trial judge serves an extremely important purpose in seeing to it that the entire system of jurisprudence has meaning. The trial judge shapes the issues, fills the record, sharpens the perimeters of the dispute, and presents the questions of law that eventually are decided by the appellate courts that create the precedents that guide us. All this in addition to applying justice to the case before him. Wyzanski pointed out that as a trial judge, he was serving his country best.

Wyzanski was the type of figure who comes about but once or twice in a lifetime. Others, less legendary, do everything mentionable and unmentionable to rise to the top. In this regard, judges are often (but fortunately not always) appointed or promoted on the basis of their friendships and alliances. Providing it is used with some degree of discretion, the appointive power, even when exercised in such a "friendly" manner, is an appropriate process, all things considered. Regardless of what theories and methods are advanced to hide the less desirable aspects of this process, no one has yet devised a better scheme. Presidents and governors, as a rule, abide by professional or ethical strictures that preclude these important judicial positions from being awarded to unqualified retainers. This, notwithstanding the classic remark of the late Republican Senator Roman Hruska of Nebraska, who, during the Haynsworth and Carswell confirmation proceedings in the early 1970s, argued in their favor that even though they were "mediocre," the mediocre people have a right to representation on the United States Supreme Court!

Sometimes, however, there are close calls. As an example, in 1973 when Reagan was governor of California, an opening on the state Supreme Court existed. Reagan had previously appointed one William Clark to the Superior Court in Ventura County. Clark was a faithful lieutenant and confidant of the Governor. He had twice failed the bar and was originally opposed by many attorneys in Ventura, but he went on from a brief career as a trial judge to a career even more brief as a judge on the California District Court of Appeals. Within a short period of time, Reagan decided to promote him to the state Supreme Court. (Ten years later, as President, Reagan would appoint him to head the National Security Council.)

Liberals and others raised quite a hue and cry over this judicial appointment which was subject by state statute to approval by a three-man body. Many lawyers and politicians, citing Clark's supposedly poor credentials, urged that the appointment be rejected. All kinds of accusations were made, and I was interested enough in the process to bring together a group of very competent attorneys to prepare a report. Clark had written some 20 published opinions (majority, dissenting and concurring) while an appellate court judge. I gave each of these attorneys copies of a number of these opinions, based upon that attorney's own expertise and familiarity with the fields of law these cases covered. Each was asked to analyze the cases he was reviewing in as objective a manner as possible, taking into consideration all factors that a scholar, practitioner and judge would deem important.

A few weeks later, each of these attorneys turned in his analysis of the cases he had reviewed. After collecting them I wrote a lengthy report, discussing each of the opinions, including Clark's analytical prowess, his perception and understanding of the case and statutory law, his writing ability and general scholarship. A few of his opinions were well written. Most, however, were written and thought through in a pedestrian manner. Two or three were badly written and poorly analyzed. Although I was not overly sympathetic to either the Governor or the appointment, I, nonetheless, concluded by stating that Judge Clark met the minimum requirements of the position he was being appointed to, adding, "if barely."

Warren Christopher who was then a leading member and official of the California bar (and later was to gain national fame and position in the Carter and Clinton administrations), having heard of my report, sought and received a copy of it. He concluded, so I understand, based in part upon the report, that neither he nor the bar should oppose the Clark appointment. Clark was confirmed; he served on that court -- adequately -- for a number of years. This is an example that in these situations involving significant appointments, most attorneys bend over backwards to try to be fair; and most chief executives take their appointive power seriously and usually make earnest efforts not to compromise the intellectual standards of the judiciary.

Yet, even when the appointment power of presidents and governors has at times come close to insulting our intelligence and sabotaging our search for justice, the system remains the best available. The British method of selecting judges may be more rational, but, given American tradition and our affinity to turn to the courts as the oracle for all of life's problems, our system is not the real rub. Tampering with the process, rather than preventing its subversion, is akin to repainting and renaming the <u>Titanic</u>.

As noted, however, political, partisan and ideological considerations, historically and inevitably, are factors rightfully influencing judicial selection. What is disturbing is that now, with the public glare upon the judiciary more pronounced, voters and those with the power of appointment require litmus tests of judicial candidates that undermine, rather than uphold, the process. Priority is now being assigned to partiality rather than independence, to agendas rather than open-mindedness, and to certainty rather than the search for justice. Judges (and arbitrators, who act in a similar capacity) often aid and abet this subversion of the process. This, too, is inevitable, for the judiciary is, when all is said and done, a human institution.

Chapter 8.

Airline I: Justice in Flight - Beyond the Wild Blue Ponder

The attorney for the discharged airline stewardess showed skill and sagacity. About halfway through what was to be a fifty-year career with a reputation as a knowledgeable, tough infighter for unions, employees and civil rights causes, this lawyer craftily wove the case for the feisty stewardess, the grievant in the arbitration. This attorney's strategy, carefully concealed through the first half of the trial, slowly emerged -- make Captain Flood the real defendant. Stewardess Ginny Meredith was portrayed as innocent as the fictional Willie Keith aboard the ill-fated <u>Caine</u>. Her lawyer, by imagination, intimation and innuendo, suggested that Meredith disobeyed the captain's orders solely because Flood was, assertedly, an imperial, drunken tyrant, incapable of giving a sensible command under trying circumstances. He was, in short, "Captain Queeg."

This newly asserted "justified mutiny," ironically, took place, according to Wouk's fictional/historical account, exactly four miles directly above the exact route the <u>Caine</u> had traversed in her near-fatal Pacific voyage during World War II, almost fifteen years before. Now, Stewardess Meredith, having been discharged by Flying Tiger Airlines for disobeying an order of Captain Flood, was seeking reinstatement, back pay and vindication. The chairman of the Arbitration Board hearing the matter was, both quaintly and improbably, a psychology professor from San Diego.

In an unusually crowded hearing room in the Los Angeles area, Meredith's lawyer was confronted with a nearly impossible assignment. That is why attorney Ruth Weyand had to resort to this dramatic, though fanciful, defense. The evidence against Meredith was overwhelming and had been meticulously and professionally presented on behalf of the airline by my firm's senior partner. I was still in law school and was not even an attorney in California at the time of the trial. But I had joined the firm just in time to read the record and write the Company's post-trial arguments. I was the brief writer. The chronicler. Ishmael.

July 2, 1958. The Constellation jet prop was filled with military personnel en route back to the States; it had departed the previous leg of its journey, Wake Island, about an hour before. The flight had been uneventful. When Captain Flood boarded the craft at Wake, he was briefed by his co-pilot on events since leaving Tokyo. Nothing unusual. Everything A-OK. "By the way, remember Mary Hayes? Well, she's aboard deadheading. Going home; her dad's passed away. I'm afraid she's been drowning her sorrows in booze and fighting sleep with seconal. She had to be practically dragged aboard. She's sloshed back there, slumped on the deck. Better keep an eye on her." Flood nodded; he recognized her problem. Not unusual in his business.

Hayes had indeed had a rough time. She was depressed, and aggravated by liquor and sedatives along the way (Tokyo, Taipei, Manila, Guam). Her condition was such that she needed help both in disembarking and reboarding at Wake. Now, with about two hours to go to Honolulu, the deadly goofballs began to take an increasing toll. Hayes, her eyes glassy, her speech slurred, her equilibrium unsteady, headed toward the navigator. She failed to make the maneuver; she collapsed in front of his seat.

Flood, hearing the ensuing commotion, turned; he immediately perceived Hayes' plight. He left his seat, turning the controls over to the co-pilot. From the official transcript, the testimony was cutting against Meredith. Flood, himself, immediately ordered oxygen to be given. This was not only in accordance with, but required by, the applicable rules and regulations of the Civil Aeronautics Board as well as the Stewardess Manual. Both not only give total authority to the captain, but direct the administration of oxygen in these situations. Flood, believing that his order was being carried out, then returned to the cockpit and ordered that the plane descend as quickly as possible:

> Q. What is the effect of the descent to 9,000 feet and the reduction of the cabin pressure to sea level?
>
> A. Well, it would give her more oxygen and we would bring our cabin down. As everybody knows here, you can die from lack of oxygen at the altitude that we were at. We were at 21,000; however, the cabin was approximately 8,700 feet. When I returned to the navigator's compartment I noticed that the mask was on the floor of the aircraft. At that time I thought that possibly Ms. Meredith knew what she was doing. I asked her if she was a registered nurse. She stated that she was not. I stated, 'I will give you a direct order to keep that oxygen mask on her until I give you permission to remove it.' She argued about it. She said, She is fighting the mask. She don't want the mask on.' I said, Nevertheless, this is a direct order. You keep the mask on her.'

Q. Then what happened after this?

A. I made the comment (to the co-pilot) that, 'I think I'm having trouble with Meredith keeping the mask on Ms. Hayes. I returned back to the navigator's compartment. The mask was again lying on the floor. So I told her, 'I thought I gave you a direct order to keep that mask on at all times.' She still continued to argue with me about it; however, she did put the mask back on. The navigator and Ms. Patterson were up there at the time and I said, 'If you're not going to comply with this order, get out of the way and let this other stewardess handle it.' She refused to get out of the way."

Richard Moran, the navigator, testified:

"I felt her hands immediately and checked her pulse. Her breathing was extremely shallow. Her pulse was very weak and her hands were cold ... I told Ms. Meredith what had happened and that I had seen Mary Hayes taking some sodium seconal capsules periodically throughout the flight. Six and a half to seven hours of the flight had elapsed by the time Ms. Hayes collapsed. Now Ms. Meredith moved into this area between the front of the seat and the back of the crew compartment bulkhead and went through a cursory analysis of what had occurred, in spite of my description... Since I saw that I was getting no response from Ms. Meredith at all, I advised Ms. Patterson to go back and get the oxygen bottle immediately with a mask and tube, the necessary paraphernalia for administering oxygen.

Ms. Patterson did. She scampered almost at a gallop back through the cabin to get the oxygen bottle. She returned with it. I took it from her. At that time Ms. Meredith had not refused to move. However, I gave her the bottle and she fumbled around with it -- I should judge five minutes elapsed -- making a very halfhearted attempt to apply it. And I looked at Ms. Patterson and she said, 'My God, she is not putting that on the girl.' So I said, 'You'd better put it on and hold it on her.'

She refused to do so, saying that she did not feel that oxygen was the proper therapy, that it should be ammonia . . . I looked forward. By this time Captain had become aware of the situation. Very briefly I gave him an analysis of what had occurred, and he said, 'Well, you have got the oxygen bottle.'

I said, 'Yes, Ms. Patterson just got the oxygen bottle.'

He said, "Well, why, isn't it being applied?'

That is when Miss Meredith stood up. She engaged Emmett in conversation that oxygen wasn't the proper therapy, that ammonia would be better. Emmett became very upset and spoke loudly to her. He said, 'Administer oxygen to her immediately, and that is an order.' He was quite emphatic. I think anybody would have understood.

> At this point Ms. Meredith turned away, stalked out the door past me and Ms. Patterson and on out the back..."

Stewardess Patterson corroborated both their testimonies, adding:

> "...Captain Flood has advised us to administer oxygen, and Ms. Meredith protested. She thought it was not the correct thing to do, and she advised administering ammonia. Captain Flood disagreed with her and commanded me to administer oxygen..."
>
> Q. Do you know what that means under those conditions?
>
> A. Yes. It would be a state of shock. I gave her oxygen..."

Following Patterson's application of oxygen, Hayes gradually regained consciousness. Soon the Constellation reached Honolulu, where an ambulance awaited. Hayes was sped to a hospital and examined. The doctor testified that but for the administration of oxygen, Hayes likely would not have survived. Flood made his report to the airline. Meredith was terminated, following review by major company officials. After internal appeals upheld the discharge, she brought the matter to arbitration.

The record showed that Meredith's initial defense was that she did not "feel" that she was disobeying the captain and that she was only doing what <u>she</u> thought was in the best interest of Hayes. This excuse -- "the well-intentioned motive" -- plainly was an extremely weak reef upon which to base a defense. Case law going back centuries, if not millennia, as well as all statutory law, makes the captain of a ship the sole, or at least the final, authority. His command is near absolute. Disobedience, regardless of intention, is virtually never condoned.

Attorney Weyand recognized that the "good intention" defense, at least by itself, would not fly. She perceived that she had to paint a picture of not only a reasonable stewardess, but an unreasonable captain. But there was absolutely nothing in the record to support an argument that Flood acted in any way irrational or that he was other than sober at all material times. Indeed, the result in this case was preordained. It was a certainty that the arbitrator had to find for the airline. A sure thing.

In the absence of facts, attorneys often resort to insinuations. Weyand elicited from Flood that he had served on the Board of Directors of the Alcohol Rehabilitation Center in San Francisco and had spent considerable time at the Rehabilitation House. She planted the seed, and it grew overnight in the mind of the arbitrator. Professors of psychology, unlike lawyers, Weyand hoped, would be less interested in demonstrable facts, such as whether Flood was an alcoholic, and more concerned with whether Meredith might have felt that Flood had alcoholic tendencies. The next day, the record reveals that Weyand had scented well:

> "The Chairman: I want to ask one question before Miss Meredith leaves the stand. This is on a topic that comes out of earlier testimony, not today's testimony.
>
> You remember, I am sure, a considerable body of testimony by Captain Flood concerning his knowledge of the effects of alcohol and barbiturates?
>
> The Witness: Yes, sir.
>
> The Chairman: I think it is fair to say that the net effect would show that he had somewhat more knowledge than the average person might have on this subject?

The Witness: Gee, I can't say yes or no on that. This is strictly based on things I heard. I knew that Captain Flood knew about alcoholism, but I had no idea he knew anything about alcohol and barbiturates mixed together.

The Chairman: You had this knowledge of which you speak at the time of the incident?

The Witness: Well, I had known it before then, yes."

Then, in her brief, Weyand seized the opening:

"Finally, Miss Meredith, by her answer to the Chairman's question as to whether at the time of the fainting incident she was aware of the Captain's knowledge of the effects of alcohol and barbiturates showed she was at the time fully aware that Captain Flood knew about alcoholism."

Weyand closed the circle, implying as though it were fact that Flood was under the influence "at the time of the incident" or that at least Meredith had good reason to believe that he was.

An arbitrator, especially in labor matters has near unlimited power; certainly, greater than a state or federal judge. An arbitrator can be dead wrong on both the law and the facts and still he can rarely be overturned. It is an anomaly in American jurisprudence, brought about by the belief that labor law, in particular, is unique, different from the law that governs society in general. This is found, primarily upon the so-called "rule of the shop," that a fairer outcome can be achieved in arbitration than in the courts because arbitrators are more familiar with, and can better ascertain, this "rule." This rule is more democratic, more attuned to the realities of the workplace, more consensual, so the proponents of arbitration believe. The rule has had a mystical life of its own.

The second major factor supporting the extension of arbitration was the realization that private legal resolution processes, such as arbitration, mediation and conciliation, must be resorted to more often, given crowded courts and the expensive, endless, and time-consuming judicial process.

In the forty-five years since the arbitration process was bestowed with such omnipotence, the tenets of the proponents of arbitration have proven partially correct. Still, in recent years, it has become increasingly clear that one of the major justifications for unrestrained arbitration -- the expertise of the arbitrator -- is now dubious. In years past, most arbitrators gained invaluable experience in the inner workings of industrial labor relations and understood and gave leadership to that sector. Today, whether dealing with ERISA, preemption, drugs, affirmative action, or in such sectors as aviation, tuna fishing, policemen's rights, baseball's free agents, computers, or other technical or esoteric fields, labor relations is quite different and usually far more sophisticated than what emerged in yesterday's smokestacked factories. At the same time, arbitrators' experience has not kept pace. For the most part, their ability and knowledge in these far-flung and often novel areas is usually not much greater than that of the average man on the street, let alone an experienced judge. Yet, they, alone, retain virtually unreviewable authority.

And the psychology professor from San Diego exercised such power in the most quixotic way. He wrote a draft opinion, which he circulated to the two management and two union members of the arbitrational panel. He had decided that the airline had discharged Meredith wrongfully, holding that she acted in good faith, presumably based upon her knowledge, including what she purportedly "knew" about Flood. Considering the circumstances, he wrote, she should not be punished. Rather, she should be reinstated. Disobedience in these situations, he stated, should be viewed with compassion. And as though they were security blankets, he coupled and colored his conclusions with customary legal citations.

Finally, in _opera bouffe_ fashion, he then verbally suggested to the management members of the panel that if they would go along with his decision and make the opinion unanimous, he would not grant Meredith back pay; otherwise he would.

Management reacted with shock to this ruling. This bordered on apoplexy when I advised them that the very authorities cited by the arbitrator, supposedly supporting his view that disobedience of this nature is at times excused by compassion, not only were inapposite to that proposition but actually undermined his legal stance! Management, moreover, could not stomach his proposed "compromise" and summarily rejected it. The chairman's decision was then made final. Meredith returned to work -- vindicated. Flood, the victim of a scarlet letter of legal sorts, returned to work -- shrouded. Just as Wouk wrote.

The Irish have a saying: Nothing is so uncertain as a sure thing.

Chapter 9.

Airline II: Justice Grounded -- Spaced Out

For the next two years, I handled a number of court and arbitration cases for Flying Tiger, most to a successful conclusion for my client. Yet I never ceased smarting about the arbitrator's misuse of his mandate in the Meredith matter. I had to grant, grudgingly, that an arbitrator's orbit transcends the law's restraints, that his quest for justice enables him to probe farther than a judge. Indeed, in 1987 the Supreme Court reaffirmed the virtual unassailable powers of arbitrators. But due process is not supposed to work the way it did in the Meredith case.

An arbitrator, like a judge, is not selected to establish his own brand of "industrial democracy." It is not his values that the parties seek; he is a hired hand, retained solely to discern and enforce the expectations of the parties. At times, of course, that assignment is extremely difficult. But aside from the succor that experience and logic accord, he can only resort to the record. Otherwise law and justice can as easily be dispensed from a slot machine. And the arbitrator's implicit findings in favor of stewardess Meredith had no rational support in the record. His "feeling" as to Flood was pure conjecture, a desperate device for an attorney, an impermissible one for a trier of fact.

* * * * *

On the morning of July 6, 1962, I flew to San Francisco to the Flying Tiger headquarters to meet with witnesses for another in a series of discharge cases that I was handling for the company. I had learned a month or two before that a pilot had threatened his superintendent with a gun; of course, he was discharged; thus the pending hearing. On the face of it, it did not appear to be an exceptional case.

A few days before my trip on this matter (which was scheduled to be tried in Los Angeles two weeks later), I finally got to open the file for the first time. In a moment, my mind began to boggle. Amidst all the correspondence and legal documents were a number of newspaper clippings which poignantly described the events that caused the discharge. From the San Mateo Times (December 23, 1960):

> "PILOT JAILED FOR KIDNAP OF SUPERIOR.
> A Flying Tiger pilot who had kidnapped his former supervisor from his Burlingame home at gunpoint was arrested at a Redwood City sanitarium late last night.
>
> His intended victim, Donald Sanders, 39, supervising pilot for Flying Tiger, escaped by jumping from the moving car and rolling behind a parked car, police said.
>
> Captain Emmett G. Flood, 43, was arrested by police at Woodside Acres Sanitarium, where he had gone for treatment after Sanders' escape.

He was returned to Burlingame and jailed on charges of assault with a deadly weapon and kidnapping and was arraigned today in Central Municipal District Court in San Mateo.

Captain Sanders said Flood came to his home and invited him outside to 'visit.'

'I didn't suspect there was anything wrong,' Sanders said. 'We had been friends for a long time, and he seemed to be calm. That was where I made my mistake.'

Sanders said Flood, a former Air Force pilot who had been with Flying Tiger for about ten years, was grounded a year ago for excessive drinking, but was reinstated last summer. He was suspended again December 1 following examinations because of emotional problems.

After Sanders got in the car, Flood started the engine and said, 'If you move, I'll blow a hole in your head.'

Flood also exhibited a .35 caliber rifle, according to the report. He didn't say where he was going or what he intended to do, other than to say he wanted to talk about his suspension.

Sanders attempted to persuade Flood that he was making a mistake. Flood started driving east on Broadway towards the Bayshore Freeway.

Just past the intersection of Broadway and El Camino Real, Flood was forced to slow the car for traffic.

Sanders hit the door lever and rolled into the street. Regaining his feet behind a parked car, Sanders ran into a restaurant and called Burlingame police. An all points bulletin was dispatched and blockades were set up throughout the Peninsula, but without success.

Shortly after 11:30 p.m., however, Flood's wife called Burlingame police and said her husband had gone to Woodside Acres and had been admitted ... (later) he was booked at Burlingame jail."

* * * * *

For the next few days I mulled over the irony of events and life's mysterious congeries. That psychology professor -- perhaps he was prescient. But he was still wrong. He went beyond his authority, legal and otherwise. His course was not just; it was simply authoritarian. Retrospectively, his "off the wall" decision was, ostensibly, defensible; but, conceivably, it affected Flood adversely. In any event, the arbitrator's exercise of power beyond that allowable in the record makes everything and everyone else powerless.

True, civilized society requires something more than that the planes run on time. It necessitates justice; but a justice reined by facts proved, not by a reign of suspicion induced by counsel and quietly confirmed by what is supposed to be a trier of fact. Derogate the defenders of justice -- due process and the rule of law -- go beyond the record, rely upon the unaccountable, then regardless of intentions, "justice" becomes unfettered flim-flam.

* * * * *

Now, here at the San Francisco Airport I had started to prepare the witnesses against Flood. Flood had no chance to prevail on the merits. The union's counsel had stated he would not even try to defend him. All he would seek was a ruling that instead of being terminated, he should have been put on sick leave at the time he was grounded at the beginning of December, eighteen months before; this would have enabled him to have gone on early pension. The Company was sympathetic and tried to cooperate, but the rules and the pension plan precluded any such leniency. The pension system apparently had no room for this particular compassion. The arbitration had to go on.

I had begun to talk to Sanders, chief pilot, at the airline hangar. We were soon interrupted by a telephone message for him. Sanders digested the words on the memo, paused, then read it to me: Flood, 44, had passed away at his home the day before. Later, I heard, he had had a liver ailment.

The arbitration hearing was postponed. The union now earnestly sought to get something for Flood's widow. The system makes exceptions, at times, for widows. The company readily agreed to a compromise and, months later, she received a modest sum. The litigation finally ground to an end.

* * * * *

Most litigated cases afford a clear-cut verdict to the impartial but perceptive observer. Some controversies, however, are far more difficult to judge. Some decisions, disturbingly, remain forever enigmatic. In this vein, I am reminded of the story of how a reigning sultan brought together all the savants in his domain.

And he told them to go away and study and analyze and write a single book that would reveal all the wisdom of the ages.

And they did so. They returned a year later and brought their sovereign such a masterful book, containing the knowledge and meaning of life.

And then the sultan said, "Now, my wise men, I want you to go away and come back and tell me about the meaning of life in but one sentence."

And they did as the sultan commanded. And they returned some time later, and on a parchment they had written: "This, too, shall pass."

And then the sultan said, "Now that you have brought me the wisdom of life in one simple sentence, go and come back and tell me the essence of it all in but one word."

And the wise men departed and some time later returned and brought to their ruler the wisdom of life reduced to a single word: "Maybe."

Chapter 10.

Clients -- O, Tempora! O, Mores!

As assiduous as they may be in seeking clients, among themselves lawyers are hardly reticent in bemoaning the difficulties, real and imagined, legal and otherwise, that clients impose upon them. Most solicitors, from their professional perches at least, tend to be condescending, if not downright unctuous, to all but a few prized clients. Still, conflicts among attorneys and clients and their causes, relating both to cross-purposes and personalities, are real. These are constant concerns that have, from the very beginning, shadowed the profession. There is no ready resolution. Each attorney must confront these problems daily and handle them primarily on an ad hoc basis. Hard and fast rules fail.

One type of conflict is often considered as having philosophical overtones, though frequently it also produces practical undertows: a critical "cause," rule or position that the lawyer is asked to advocate or oppose and about which he and his client, for whatever reason, strongly disagree. At times, and with honor, attorneys will reject representation in such actions; it is deemed a "no-win" dilemma. To put forth one's best effort to achieve an end that is anathema personally or devastating professionally borders on the masochistic.

Many dedicated and devoted practitioners nonetheless have been able to brook such misjoinders. The Jewish lawyer who defends the Nazi marches in Skokie has his counterpart in John Adams, who, in 1770, represented Captain Preston, the main defendant in the Boston Massacre. The defendants' lawyers in each of these cases tested in the crucible of the courts the "majesty" of the law despite their "blood," their neighbors' wrath, and the threat to their own personal and professional security. And privately they continued to champion causes contrary to the causes of their clients.

More often, however, the conflict resolves itself on practical realities. One who daily represents management in labor law, for example, can hardly bounce back and forth to speak on behalf of unions before the same courts.[8] In the eminent domain field, those who advocate on behalf of property owners as a specialty are compromising themselves and undermining their clients from both sides -- by also becoming attorneys for condemning authorities. The challenge may be intriguing, but in these fields,

---

[8] Interestingly, in the geographic area of my practice, there are numerous attorneys, like myself, who represent management, exclusively, in labor relations -- despite the fact that ostensibly these lawyers are politically often allied with, or sympathetic to, the "other side." We are repeatedly asked about this anomaly. For myself, I believe in a viable, non-monopolistic, competitive free enterprise system. Unions, if restrained from monopolistic activities, have every right to sell their product, labor, in the marketplace (even at times militantly); and management has every right to protect itself. Neither has a monopoly on virtue or vice; nor should either have one on might.

as in many others, a lawyer cannot in the same time frame, urge upon the courts contrary legal positions and do so effectively. If a lawyer's ego or pocketbook clouds his vision, his clients, on this subject, are usually not so self-deceptive.

The foregoing problems are fairly well recognized. More subtle are the subjective conflicts. Sometimes they are not even discerned by the client or the attorney. They can be found, and flounder upon, such unlikely factors as age, race, sex, or religion. More probable, conflicts may stem from personality traits -- too gregarious or insufficiently so; tight-lipped or loquacious; highbrow or hoi polloi; condescending or patronizing; trusting or suspicious; overbearing or milquetoast. The whole gamut of factors that create or undermine mutual trust in all human relations, comes into play.

Admittedly, there are situations where the personal conflicts between an attorney and his client will have very little or no effect on the outcome of the issue that brought them together. Often, however, the lack of trust rankles; neither the attorney probes nor the client opens up sufficiently. Each unconsciously suspects the other, and both plod singly along harm's way. At times, this manifests itself in strained communication, resulting in ineffective preparation and presentation of the case. Too often, this psychological conflict causes the client to ignore the advice he pays for or blinds the attorney to the client's needs. When such strains continue, the relationship is best terminated, if possible. Otherwise, everyone, justice most of all, suffers.

Time and custom, themselves, create conflict. Given the mach-like velocity of change in society in the past generation, it might be expected that lawyers, trained and versed in sturdy and ancient institutions, would find a chasm between their more modern-minded clients and the comfortable cloister they have created for themselves. (And that seems to be the case, as will be described later.) There are exceptions, of course. Sometimes it is the client, not the lawyer, who is the atavist, the specter from the past. Let me tell you about one such icon character ...

... Of Troglodytes and Guns ...

Much of what I know about the late D.B. Lewis is merely lore, but what I relate as to my dealings with him is fact, if fantastic. D.B. Lewis was a fairly well-known character, a man of importance in his time (1945-1965) here in Southern California. When I met him in the early 1960's, he was a distinguished-looking, gray-haired man, handsome in appearance and courtly in manner. Apparently starting with nothing more than determination and a Horatio Alger belief in the free enterprise system, having been born in that era, he emerged soon after World War II as a very successful manufacturer and businessman. From almost nothing, he created a near monopoly in -- of all things -- dog food.

Soon after World War II, Lewis, as the owner and producer of Dr. Ross Dog Food, had captured much of the canned dog food market on the West Coast and had emerged as an independent operator of considerable importance in the field. In the process he had become extremely wealthy, so much so, or so I have been told, that in the early 1950's when his wealth had become abundant (I got the impression that he really didn't care about money per se), his attention was devoted to the championing of conservative causes. With a winsome, almost childish sincerity, he espoused the free enterprise system as a religious crusade. As an original right-wing ideologue, he fervently loved the United States; with equal fervor he abhorred its government, which he delightedly challenged in a number of ways. He reveled in taking out full-page newspaper advertisements on behalf of Dr. Ross Dog Food, attacking the social policies of the federal government and its seeming failure to develop effective anti-Communist doctrine. From his point of view this was perfectly proper, particularly since the government was then taxing him in the 90% bracket and therefore was paying for 90% of these advertisements. Years later, the deductibility of these expenses for tax purposes itself became a major legal question in which he challenged the bureaucracy.

During the 1950's, it is told, he asserted with disarming frankness that the only way he or anyone could change American foreign policy was to go to the very heart of the problem and get control of the atom bomb! Apparently he bought up huge parcels of property in the Nevada desert containing the source of U-235, at that time the most significant element in the production of atomic energy. Unfortunately for him (and fortunately for the Soviet Union, the United States, and the rest of the world), U-235 soon thereafter became far less scientifically critical in the effectuation of nuclear power. Thwarted in this manner from materially affecting civilization, he then turned his attention to and became one of the original and major benefactors of the John Birch Society, purportedly donating large amounts of money to its cause and certainly giving a good deal of his talent and time to its programs. Indeed, in the 1960's he caused quite a stir by donating $1,000,000 to Pepperdine College to establish a chair for Dan Smoot, a leading columnist, writer, and theoretician of the John Birch Society. Of course, the $1,000,000 was given only on the condition that Dan Smoot be appointed the first professor to the chair. Again unfortunately for D.B., this bequest received such criticism throughout the country that Pepperdine found it necessary to turn down the gift, reluctantly.

But D.B. -- whatever his critics might have thought of him and whatever the public image he created for himself -- was nonetheless a near genius a la Henry Ford. Like Ford, he had dynamic vision, a scientific bent, indefatigable drive, unusual business acumen, and advertising daring. All this coupled with a down-home philosophy, a messianic and personal foreign policy, and an aversion to foreigners. Like Ford, the assembly line was his engine for all else.

He created his dog food factory, a relic combination of Dickens and Rube Goldberg, on the east side of Los Angeles. It may have originally been set up as a replica of the Alamo some time between the Mexican-American and the Civil War. This three-story, add-on factory had all varieties of pipes and tubes and spouts and chutes and pulleys and ladders and hoists and belts and tunnels going through, under, atop and around its walls, ceilings, floors, stairwells, attics, alcoves, niches, notches and cellars, making it look like the backdrop for "Modern Times." For D.B. not only devised this workable monstrosity, he ran it, albeit in Shogun style, as though it were the Chocolate Factory. He knew the composition of each of the numerous flavors of dog food that he created, and enjoyed being tested by identifying them by taste while blindfolded.

Fittingly, he was a frugal and very unostentatious man. He did not stand on ceremony and said what was on his mind. And said it in such a gentle and polite manner that he gave the appearance of a don at an English private school, a Mr. Chips. There was no red carpet in, or ivy on, his nonconforming use structure. To get to his office, you would climb up three flights of rickety stairs that clearly had not been swept since the Korean Conflict, over a decade before. The reception room -- if it could be called such -- had in it solely one piece of furniture, which vendors and others would use at their risk. This sofa had three cushions, each one of which had a rusty spring in the center -- exposed and waiting. So much for salesmen.

But D.B.'s own office across a narrow hall was scarcely any more opulent. Its nineteenth century rolltop desk was not there for picturesque purposes. Strewn about the 10' x 12' space occupied by this millionaire were all sorts and varieties of invoices, sales brochures, political tracts and correspondence, unfiled, undated, and unsorted. There were two chairs -- one for D.B. and one for his listener. The ambience of this room was illuminated by D.B.'s shining countenance and a single uncovered light bulb dangling on a cord from the paint-chipped ceiling. The rest of the room was adorned only with dust; his many awards and scrolls were nowhere in sight. This was his domain, his fiefdom. In that structure some 120 workers concocted and canned dog food. All of them except D.B.'s older brother, as near as I could ascertain, were Mexican-Americans. Many had made their trek north only months before. Most of them had but a limited knowledge of English, if any. In the 1960's, when I was introduced to this incongruity, all of them were earning close to minimum wage; that is, all except D.B.'s older brother, who as foreman was purportedly making approximately $5 an hour. In B.B.'s will, wherein he left millions to right-wing causes and charities, he left his wife $1,000 per month. This legacy, however, had a stipulation: if she earned any money, such amounts were to be deducted from the monthly stipend! Perhaps the <u>coup</u> <u>de</u> <u>grace</u> provision of his will was the bequest of $1,500,000 to establish an organization to be called "The Defenders of Liberty." This was to be the conservative counterpart of the ACLU. It had two peculiar restrictions, however. It could only defend the Constitution as it stood in 1950 (whatever that was)! In addition, it could not defend anyone who resorted to making use of the Constitution's Fifth Amendment! (Ollie North was still a boyscout.)

My dealings with D.B. came about by pure chance, having nothing to do with social kinship. My firm had represented him in many endeavors, primarily in his tax fights with the government and more recently in an attempt to defeat an organizational drive by the Butchers' Union, which sought to represent all the Mexican-American workers at his plant. In the midst of this organizational campaign, the senior partner who was handling the matter retired somewhat abruptly; he turned over the union organization problem to me. No one else was available. This was early in 1964, and I had been in the practice of labor law but two or three years. D.B.-type personalities were not familiar to me. This was to be my baptism from the right.

I quickly appraised the situation, and concluded that the only possible hope (prayer) for this company to win an NLRB election would be if the unit -- those eligible to vote -- were extended beyond the 120 workers who toiled in the factory. I ascertained that there were 40 salesmen employed by the company who journeyed throughout the western United States. None of them ever reported to the factory or had anything to do with the factory; indeed, probably all but one or two had never even seen the place. Still, we had to have them within the unit nonetheless.

Under Board law, there was no "community of interest" between the roving salesmen and the workers in the plant, and any attempt to join them would surely have been rejected by the Board if the union opposed their inclusion. I formally requested that the union include them. The union attorney appraised the situation and readily agreed that the salesmen could be included in the unit. It soon became apparent why the union counsel was so accommodating. The union had 120 votes wrapped up tight and could easily afford to include the 40 salesmen in the voting, rather than have me resort to what it would assume would be delaying tactics. No one had any doubt as to where the 40 salesmen's votes would go. They were going to be flown in from all over the country to see the factory for the first time and to vote -- the "American way."

In a valiant but knowingly futile attempt to "turn around" a number of union voters to support the company's position, I met with D.B. in his office and laid out a campaign by which he would seek the support of the workers. It was basically a soft sell by him, to convince the workers that if he had not done what he should for them, he had seen the light and would, in the most general terms, try to improve. I realized that this self-critical "line" was inimical to D.B., but saw no other alternative; and I laid it out for him as delicately and diplomatically as possible.

This old man did not bite. He saw it for what it was, to wit, something less than standing tall in the saddle. And he put me in my place. "Now listen, Sammy," he said in the most soothing tone, "I'm going to talk to them *my* way. I'm going to bring them all together and tell them quite frankly that they should vote against the Commies. I'll tell them they're a bunch of immigrants who don't know what this country is about, and that I'll do what's right for them. They'll listen to me because they love me and trust me. And I'll tell them what a great thing it is to be an American, and they'll listen because they're Mexicans and they all want to be Americans," adding, "and they like their jobs." Clearly, he was anxious to march off to the lists. There, he was sure, justice, as he saw it, would triumph.

I stared at D.B., with his shining, beatific visage and twinkling blue eyes, and I was as confounded as ever. I realized that I could not sway him completely but might only try to tone down what would otherwise likely be unfair labor practices as distinguished from just incredible gaffes. Despite my urgings, he later spoke to the assembled employees; I was informed that he gave them the same philippic he had voiced to me. It was received by them in much the same manner as the King of Id's subjects feign interest in their sovereign's latest pontifical spiels.

On the day of the election I returned to the animal factory, climbed the picaresque stairway, crossed the unique reception room, and entered D.B.'s century-old citadel. The union attorney had been waiting for me. We worked out the terms of the election which was just about to begin in the employees' coffee room, and soon thereafter the voting commenced. I went back to D.B.'s office and the union attorney adjourned to a vacant room, all of us awaiting the conclusion and result of the secret ballot election which would be over in an hour.

D.B. and I, not exactly exuding <u>bonhomie</u>, nonetheless found a common bond. I respected his sincerity and basic honesty. He apparently respected my ability and perhaps something else. Thus, there was some mutual respect. D.B. started to fidget. He did not know what to do with the time he had to wait. Obviously, D.B., like me, could not psychologically abide to waste time. So he picked up a political tract written by Dan Smoot and handed it to me. The article was about gun control. This was some 5-6 months after the assassination of President Kennedy, and the gun control issue had become a major one in the country.

Before Congress there was a bill to restrict the sale of guns; the fight was being waged in prolonged debate in the Senate at that time. The opponents of gun control were up in arms over the possibility of this legislation -- limited as it was -- passing Congress. The John Birch Society and others on the right of the American political spectrum were lobbying intently to defeat this gun control legislation. D.B. was emotionally and financially in the throes of that battle. But thinking that I was a "reasonable" man (after all, I was defending his interests), he asked me to read the Smoot article, which I readily did.

He watched me carefully and with expectant approval as I appeared to take interest in the article. Actually, the article was reasonable and logical, if one accepted its premises. It basically defended the proposition that there should be no restrictions on the sale of guns, on the essentially correct position that such legislation would not really prevent criminals from obtaining guns.

When I finished reading it, D.B. looked at me and said, "Well, Sammy, what do you think?" I scrutinized the yellowing light bulb and then turned to him and said, "Mr. Lewis, I agree with Smoot's argument that this gun control legislation is not going to keep guns away from criminals," and then I paused. D.B. brightened up -- at last, a convert from the left! But before he could inhale such a conquest, I added what would appear to have been an obvious consideration. "I am concerned, however, sir," I said in the most respectful tone I could marshal, "that 14- and 15-year-old kids will get hold of these guns and kill people by accident."

D.B. looked puzzled, as though this argument had never before been raised; it seemed to surprise him. But he soon gathered his wits. He looked me straight in the eye and in reply to my concern said in dead seriousness, "Well, if we didn't have these child labor laws, the 14- and 15-year-old kids would be in the factories where they should be."

I do not know how or why I wandered there, but some minutes afterwards I was talking to the union attorney privately in a hidden alcove of the building. I repeated to him what my client had just said to me. I told it to him in near disbelief. The union attorney had been around longer than I and accepted Lewis simply as a fact of life. He shrugged his shoulders and said, "You take your clients as they come."

* * * * *

Soon thereafter the ballots were tallied. As I recall, the vote was -- 118 ("yes") for the union, 40 ("no") for the company. There were two challenged ballots, both voters having written across them. On one, the scrawling was indecipherable. On the other, the employee had written, either phonetically or philosophically, "See!"

* * * * *

Despite the illiterate lance tossed out in an uncertain direction by this anonymous employee, fairness compels history to record that D.B. took the election results, I thought, with equanimity. The struggle, perhaps he thought, had just begun. This authentic American kamikaze passed away almost two years later. Though he had seemingly bargained with the union in good faith, he still, I recall, hadn't signed a labor agreement. Soon afterwards, the Dr. Ross money-machine, itself, became a memory.

Chapter 11.

Where There's A Will, There's A Gay

There are occasions when the law leads. In these situations the public follows -- perhaps enthusiastically, more often passively, but frequently grudgingly or even defiantly. We all have witnessed in the civil rights field the profound effect that court decisions and later statutory laws have had in remolding society's mores. To a lesser extent this phenomenon -- the law's moral force -- has fostered the stunning success of the feminist movement, enabling a literal majority population, through the application of "minority rights," to aspire to be a majority. Yet even when the timing has been propitious, as in the foregoing epochs, deeply ingrained mores have not been easily altered by fiat. The fact that such viscerally held beliefs and ways of life can be changed at all, albeit with lingering resistance, demonstrates that, although our society is loosening its moorings from the rule of law, there is still a powerful reservoir of respect for that anchor that makes liberty possible.

Generally, however, the law simply follows. The public, through myriad mutations, senses, stirs, and then moves in a certain direction. Lawmakers -- legislatures and courts -- try to keep pace, impediments slow them down. A critical time lag results. If the courts or legislatures move before public opinion jells, or go in a different direction, the public can be vindictive. If, on the other hand, the lawmakers are too slow in "coming around," are not in tow, law and society are "out of sync."

This hysteresis causes problems: timing, so critical in most human endeavors, is paramount in law. The law, however, is constantly feuding with its times. Lawyers can never be certain of their footing; precedents -- the underpinnings of the profession -- often are illusory in the face of a judge's understanding and application of today's mores -- his or the public's.

A story told about federal district Judge Charles Wyzanski, Jr. underscores this point. As a young attorney during the early days of the New Deal, he gained the admiration of the sophisticated legal community in Washington. In 1937 he was appointed Solicitor of the Department of Labor, where he successfully argued before the Supreme Court the constitutionality of the Social Security Act and the National Labor Relations Act, among other cases. Though Wyzanski's triumphs were unquestionably impressive, they occurred at the critical juncture in the Court's history when the "stitch in time saved nine." The Court, in response to the political and economic exigencies of the day, had shifted its position and now gave constitutional sanction to New Deal legislation. In responding to the congratulations of his friends and peers for his string of victories before the Court, Wyzanski was both wag and sage. "The cases," he said, "were won not by Mr. Wyzanski, but by Mr. Zeitgeist."

The 1960's were neither the best of times nor the worst of times. But they were, by all accounts, a time out of kilter. What had gone before no longer fit; what came after seemed tentative and remained fretfully indistinct. In such a setting, law became an uncertain trumpet. Usually we turn to the law, the most earthly institution, to be the conduit for preserving and at times molding society's mores. When in focus, it is also a mirror for reflecting those mores. But the gap between the practice and the state of the law in the decade of the Sixties was boggling. This chasm manifested itself in the most salient of cultural and social intercourse -- sex and language. Sometimes these two life forces move at a different gait; more often, they change in concert.

First things first -- sex. Since the rise of the middle class in the Western world, the prevailing sexual mores have generally been those "rules" that that class imposes on itself. By and large, as Shaw and others have so shamelessly shown us, these scriptures of the middle class are barely given lip service by the lower or upper classes. In the Sixties, it was the middle class that brought about a sexual revolution; no one now over 50 needs further edification, even if, like myself, they still have barely reached the semi-emancipated stage. Lawyers were not immune to this onslaught, most of them were either defending or storming the barricades.

The sexual zeitgeist of the Sixties came home to me with a thud, in a legal context, at the middle of that decade. For a number of years I had as a client and friend one William Warren Whitney, a scion of the famous American family, some ten years my junior. His age better enabled him to rent and openly share a quaint love nest in Laguna Beach with his then favorite lady. From that checkpoint WWW would hop, skip and jump all over the world in handling his investments and passions. During these frequent sojourns he would leave whatever unattended business he had for me to attend to, including his plumbing problems at his perch on the beach, and dealing with and placating the owner of that property, one Lester Flack.

I never actually met Mr. Flack. On numerous occasions, however, I communicated with him concerning WWW, both by letter and telephone. His stationery was flowery; his voice over the phone had an unusual lilt. Neither of these expressions of personality, in my naivete, meant a thing to me. (Indeed, on that score, someone a few years later witnessed me following a beautiful vision for two city blocks, enraptured by such exquisite femininity, only to be later told that the enticing creature I was tracking was a transvestite!) To this day, I do not know what Flack looks like. Our dealings were strictly at a distance and solely concerned WWW's tardy payments of rent and assessments, stray cats and friends, defective plumbing, and the like. But I shall never forget Mr. Flack.

My secretary buzzed me. "A Mr. Lester Flack on the phone, wants to know if you're busy. If so, he'll call back." Will was in South America somewhere. What had he failed to do now? What was Flack complaining about this week? I took the call.

"Hello, Mr. Tobin. I hope I'm not interrupting, but it truly is a matter of importance."

"What has my client done now, Mr. Flack?"

"Oh, it's not William I'm calling about. It is I. It's personal."

Strange, what could be personal between us, I thought. "What do you mean, Mr. Flack?" I asked, somewhat hesitantly.

Slightly taken aback by my possibly misinterpreting his "personal" for "intimate," Flack was quick to respond, "It's a legal matter. William speaks so highly of you, and I do need a good lawyer."

He then went on to describe his legal Megillah. What he recounted jarred me, for his relating the story to me was like a round hole trying to get into a square peg. I may have, as a consequence, missed some of his telling remarks, but what I clearly heard was telling enough. It seemed that Flack felt he'd been "had" by someone with whom he had had a long, personal, and trusting relationship. And this friend was now dead. Flack had lived with this man, off and on, for many years; he was about 70 when he died the previous week. On the day before he called me, Flack learned that he had been "cheated" by his friend. Despite long-standing promises over these many years, the deceased had failed to leave anything in his will to Flack, to compensate him for what Flack described as "personal services."

The man left his entire estate to his 94-year-old mother! Flack was seeking justice, pure and simple.

At this point, I was still unclear as to what Flack was claiming or how he had been cheated or whether or how he intended to overturn the will. I started by pointing out to him that even if there were grounds to contest the will in probate (either because the decedent had been incompetent or had been coerced at the time he executed it), unless another will were found that provided for Flack, the decedent's entire estate would almost surely go to his nearest heir (presumably his elderly mother) and that Flack had nothing to gain by having the will rejected by the courts. I then suggested that whatever recovery or recourse Flack had would be to sue the decedent's estate for contractual rights, for services rendered to his friend while he was alive. Was there a contract? Could it be proven? Was it valid? What was the "consideration" for the promise to pay, that is, what were the services performed? Was there a statute of limitations involved? The Statute of Frauds?

Since this area of the law was far from my specialty, I was slightly daunted and proceeded cautiously. I suspected at this point that the services Flack mentioned were in the nature of being a personal valet to this gentleman. But to be certain, I directly asked him to describe to me the nature of these services for which he now sought compensation. There was a pause, and then Flack answered' "I'm a homosexual. That's the way I serviced him." From my end of the phone came a gulp, a gasp, and a long silence . . .

No question about it, I was clearly out of my element.

The only other "for-sure" in this unreal world was that I needed help. Regaining a modicum of composure, I muttered to Flack that I would have to consult with experts in my firm and would call him back soon. I immediately sought aid from what I then perceived to be a seemingly unlikely but correct source. Heading the firm's probate department at that time was a rising young Establishment-type attorney, Jonathan Ordway. I hoped that he would help to extricate me from this delicate discomfiture.

I camped in Jon's office and told him about my telephone conversation with Flack, implying that there was only one proper course a prestigious downtown law firm such as ours could take: get rid of L. Flack, delicately, diplomatically, but with dispatch. Further, the expert, my junior partner Jon, the Pasadena paragon, should call Flack and summarily but professionally direct him to seek counsel elsewhere, presumably on the western fringes of our town.

I figured wrong. I forgot the generation gap, which existed in Jon's San Marino enclave as it exists almost everywhere. Jon listened to my troubled tale with aplomb. He said we ought to call Flack and pursue the course of inquiry. While agreeing with my quick analysis of the legal pitfalls in the case, Jon, ten years my junior, was far from judgmental -- indeed, he was philosophical. He expressed interest in pursuing the possibility of suing the estate for the value of Flack's services, knowing full well, and seemingly unfazed by, the illicit nature of these services. "My God," I said to myself, "Jon's actually considering our representing this character in court! He couldn't be; he's just pulling my leg!

Ambivalence now took over. Uncertain of Jon's real intent, I decided to go along for the ride. While we were in the process of telephoning Flack in Laguna and talking to him on "the box," Jon and I, in the "good ol' boy" manner, snickered at Flack's plight and our conceivable involvement. On my part, my laughter was edged with nervousness, or vice versa. Sensing this, Jon knavishly suggested that I was a stodgy square steeped in the arcane. Feebly, I rejoined by accusing him of being a closet Democrat. Before this banter became pathetic, however, Flack came on the line. I introduced Jon to him and then asked Flack to start at the beginning, so to speak, and in reasonable detail describe the relationship between him and his late "employer."

After repeating and elaborating upon what he had previously told me, taking full license with his language, Flack then pointedly asked if we would take his case and what were his prospects of prevailing. Jon seized the reins. After ascertaining from Flack that a handsome sum was involved, Jon went to the core considerations.

"Mr. Flack," Jon said, 'the only realistic way you could be compensated for your services ... by the way, how long did you perform these services?"

"About fifteen years," Flack responded.

"Well, as I was saying, for your lawyer to be able to win a judgment in your favor, it will have to be on the basis of your having a contract with your friend... ah, patron. Obviously, this contract wasn't in writing... unless there were letters between you that memorialized his promises to you. Were there?"

"Oh, yes. I'm sure many, many of his letters to me, all of which I have kept, contain this promise," Flack enthusiastically said.

"Good!" Jon exclaimed. "That should get us by the statute of frauds problem and ease the period of limitations, and corroborating witnesses will not be essential."

I noted with concern that Jon's interest was being whetted. He went on. "Of course, there will be a problem in evaluating your services. Do you, Lester, have any idea of how we, you, can value them?"

Flack thought for a moment. "He told me in the last few years that I was getting better and better and that he was enjoying it more and more," he proudly stated.

At this point, torn between laughing out loud and being panicked that Jon might not be just stringing Flack along, I signaled to him by hand to cut off this bizarre conversation. Jon ignored me and went on.

"Les," he said, "since no figure was ever put on the value of your services, we'll have to proceed... ah, if we take the case ... on what we lawyers call 'quantum meruit.' What that means is that you get compensated based upon what those services are worth in the, ah, market. That might mean getting some comparative data and perhaps an expert or two."

Frantically, I waved my arms. Jon was satisfied that this was now an appropriate point to hear me out. He asked Flack if we could put him "on hold" for a minute, as we had to check out a matter briefly. Flack agreed, and the "hold" button was hit.

"C'mon, Jon. You must be putting me on. I might be square," I declared, "but I know one thing for sure. This law firm will not take this case. There is no way in the world that an attorney from this firm is going to stand in front of a jury and say, 'On behalf of my client, the cocksucker...'"

A wry smile crossed Jon's face. "I guess you're right, Stan, but not entirely for the reason that concerns you. Let me shortcut this," he added, putting Flack back on "the box."

"Sorry to keep you waiting, Mr. Flack," Jon said. "We were thinking, since the attorneys' fees in this matter won't come out of the estate in probate, your cost to litigate this matter may be very high. And because of the very speculative nature of your case, we couldn't, of course, take it on a contingency fee basis."

Jon had, indeed, shortcutted the matter. He had, in the parlance of the law, really gone "to the essentials." Wanly, Flack indicated that he was not in a position to pay our retainer or hourly fees. Jon, however, properly felt and expressed to Flack that we had a professional duty of sorts to give Flack some free legal guidance. He then proceeded to advise Flack that the best avenue of recourse was to discuss the matter with the deceased's mother and, especially, her attorney, and, on his own, suggest to them that it would be in the best interest of her and the memory of the deceased that some out-of-court settlement be reached.

I chirped in with one or two related suggestions, and after five or ten minutes of our explaining the strategy and legal points, Flack seemed quite satisfied and was prepared to pursue our recommendations. The conversation ended on that gratifying note. I never spoke to Flack again, although I later learned that he had reached some kind of settlement with the nonagenarian heir along the lines we had presented to him.

After Jon put down the phone, we shared smiles. Curious as to what had motivated Jon to take the stance he did, I inquired if he had seriously entertained the idea of our representing Flack. "Not really," Jon responded. "But it would have been most interesting. We're on the verge of great social change in this country. In a decade or two, this case may not be so unusual. What seems weird to most of us today may be normal tomorrow. The things that the Pill and new-fangled concepts of freedom have brought about will make the probate court in the years ahead look like a continuing soap opera, and I don't mean just traditional greed. Why, some day soon someone like Flack will sue -- successfully -- in probate based upon his quasi-spousal relationship with Mr. Whoever and his being wrongfully cut out of the will. Especially in this community property state with these liberal judges -- your friends!"

We mused over these new wives' tales and then Jon said, "One thing's sure, Stan. You older lawyers, [pointing his finger; I was still in my mid-thirties] are going to have to learn to stop playing Hamlet with your prospective clients. You don't have to agree with them or even like them. Take them as they come."

* * * * *

In over three decades that have passed since then, much of what Jon had foreseen has come to pass. And introspection, if not wisdom, comes with age. Did I act appropriately, or did I simply take the easy way out in rebuffing the opportunity to represent Flack in his attempt to obtain justice? I did not so view his aim then; yet, at least by present-day standards, he had a viable cause of action. His friend may well have treated him unjustly, both in fact and in law. Thus, the irony of this incident is, in part, that frequently the law itself is a barrier to justice. Here, it was not really the law, but mores, that stood in the way.

If Flack came into our offices today, I would, nonetheless, probably again spurn representing him on such a matter. It would not be simply because mine is a straitlaced firm that even now, as a stated matter of policy, will rarely handle even divorce cases; nor would it be on account of the fact that a number of my partners would strongly oppose any involvement in such litigation. It would mainly be because of my own shortcomings. I would feel uncomfortable urging his case. All lawyers have limitations, both in ability and in character. Other available lawyers would not be handicapped in Flack's case. I would. Only if he had difficulty obtaining competent counsel, capable of undertaking his cause with -- in the language of the old Canons of Professional Ethics -- "warm zeal," would I feel it necessary to ignore my own discomfort.

Chapter 12.

__Language and the Law: Of Slag and Slugs__

If lawyers of my generation are taken aback professionally by the generation gap in regard to sexual mores, they witness a similar cultural shock in the use (or non-use) of language. These two vitalities generally travel in tandem; liberal fashion allowed one is accompanied by equal freedom accorded the other. Likewise, constraint. In a broader view, however, language is more than a reflection of the mores (or even the morality) of the times. It is especially intrinsic to law, and thus, in part, to the quest for justice.

Semantics, clearly, are at the heart of many legal disputes. Admittedly, most cases are not decided by the niceties or vagaries of words. Torts, domestic relations, and crimes constitute the bulk of lawsuits, and these matters generally do not turn upon a narrow or confusing import of words or phrases. But in other areas of the law -- contracts, commercial disputes, wills, taxation -- and especially in the interpretation and implementation of statutes, words and their exact meanings are very often at the crux of the controversy.

Lawyers have been criticized, to put it mildly, for being unnecessarily engrossed with, and deliberately pedantic in, their use of language. They appear to obfuscate rather than clarify. Periodically, the cry goes out, even from such luminaries as Edwin Newman and William Safire, to require all laws and governmental dockets to be written in "simple" language. It is almost universally believed that the highfalutin language that lawyers employ is totally unnecessary and exists solely to justify the lawyer's existence (or fee). Unfortunately, this is one of those self-satisfying myths that has less in reality to commend it than meets the eye.

Too often, admittedly, lawyers twist language for swarthy gain. And more often than they care to admit, many $200-an-hour lawyers can't write worth a tinker's dam. It is also true that language frequently is made undoubtedly complex in the legal context. And, like doctors writing prescriptions, many lawyers derive inordinate satisfaction from the mystique of the language they employ. In a good many instances, esoteric language with excessive verbiage is used to disguise the absence of clear thought.

On the other hand, the near obsession to simplify language in the legal context is usually unjustified. Despite the genuineness of its genesis, it is often a hobgoblin. Language, the most important factor separating homo sapiens from the rest of the animal kingdom, is a reflection of the complexities of civilized society. "High thoughts," as Aristophanes wrote, "must have high language." The more advanced the society, the more need for an expansive language. The more complicated the issue, the greater the need for exactness in expression. Law is complex; wishing it otherwise will not make it so.

This appeal by commentators, scholars and politicians to simplify the language of the law naturally finds a receptive public. To tear off the mask of verbiage, however, will not necessarily bring about the simplicity and understanding features its proponents envision. Some years ago, the Stanford Law Review put this issue to a test. As an experiment, it took a typical law review article and sought to reduce it to so-called "plain talk." The article as it was written -- to communicate within the legal field -- was rated "very difficult," scoring a 6.5 rating on the "Flesch" scale (named after Rudolph Flesch of the "art of plain talking" fame). The first attempt to make it more readable reduced that rating to 4.8, termed "fairly difficult." The result of this first effort did improve readability without sacrificing substance. A second attempt to simplify the article brought about a 2.3 rating by the Flesch score, now "fairly easy." But the price to achieve that level of understanding was obviously high. Why? Because now it hardly made any sense to the lawyers (the more Flesch, the less meat). As the Law Review editors noted, "When you are writing for experts, extreme simplicity fails to convey meaning. Furthermore, the low score made it no more understandable to laymen without a college education." The Law Review concluded that laymen were as puzzled as they had been by previous drafts. Interestingly enough, that study and conclusion was done almost 50 years ago, long before the language proficiency of the average American high school graduate began to plummet.

If experience is the life of the law, language is its force. As bewildering as the language of the law may be to the uninitiated, as aggravating as the bafflement of the generation gap is to those so engulfed, the environmental or geographical gap is still another communication barrier interfering with the pursuit of justice. In any one society, there are widely divergent uses of everyday language, reflecting important differences in cultural values. Lawyers and judges frequently err in using language that presumably reflects shared values but which, in reality, expresses different meanings or values than those which many others in the same or kindred society understand or share. This communication or cultural fault can lead to comical ends or to serious injustices.

Lawyers must be wary of traps that ensnare them when they innocently project their own cultural mores to their clients and others -- children of another time or products of another place. Language is frequently the trip cord. I was to learn this lesson the hard way. This particular situation highlighted the consequences that can arise when communication becomes clouded by cultural, as distinguished from semantic, barriers.

In the midst of Southern California's "Inland Empire," at the edge of the Lower Desert, was once the domicile of the Etiwanda Steel Company. It was an unimposing but complete steel mill that had been in business for many years; it had long been a client of my law firm. I had been handling its labor-management legal matters, frequenting the plant trying to put out fires -- strikes, slowdowns, heated disputes. The infernal nature of the mill insured never-ending fracas and contention. (Indeed, the Kaiser Steel Mills in the same general vicinity have had the unenviable national reputation, for decades, of being in perpetual grievance and arbitration proceedings.)

The particular case involved a fight; in a steel plant, that's a run-of-the-mill happening. This one had an unusual twist, however. Charles Harden was a supervisor for the company. He had had an ongoing feud with an employee in his crew, Chip McCoy. Harden, born and raised in Bessemer, Alabama, had literally grown up in a steel mill. McCoy, from Oklahoma, made the trek to California when he was a kid during the great migration of the 1930's, and was just now, in 1965, finishing his apprenticeship. Somehow or other these two men never hit it off well. This time, both went too far.

Harden for much of that hot summer day had been complaining to McCoy that his work with the slag was sloppy and that he appeared to be slacking off. McCoy did not take this criticism gladly and soon built up his own head of steam. When he had reached the boiling point during another verbal exchange,

McCoy, only a couple of feet away from Harden, shouted at him, "Fuck you, you son of a bitch!" Instinctively, Harden smacked him on the jaw, cleanly breaking it. Eight months later, at the time of the trial, McCoy's jaw was still in wires.

The company discharged both Harden and McCoy the next day: Harden, because supervisors are not paid to break jaws; McCoy, because the evidence plainly showed that he had instigated the altercation. Harden resigned himself to his termination because, realistically, he had no choice. Supervisors are not covered by the collective bargaining agreement, and thus he would not be able to have management's decision overturned in arbitration. McCoy could lick his wounds, so to speak; he chose to fight it out before an arbitrator.

In preparing the company's case against McCoy, it was clear that the crux of the defense was that he had started the fight by resorting to, in labor law parlance, "fighting words." Case law was overwhelming that such conduct justified that the linguistic instigator suffer the consequences of his rhetoric -- discharge -- in addition to whatever physical punishment he may have brought upon himself.

I read, in 1987, where an arbitrator, in a modern version of "On The Waterfront," refused to uphold the discharge of a stevedore who, in order to effectively end an argument, pasted his superior -- the reverse of the Harden-McCoy bout. The arbitrator opined that resort to fisticuffs in that industry was to be expected, must be considered acceptable conduct in that environment, and, a fortiori, condonable. Perhaps, he implied, aggravated assault would be enjoined!

When I first reflected on that jarring case, I concluded that that decision was an aberration, or, at the least, the arbitrator was avant garde. About a year later, however, I was agog when I read that a three-judge federal circuit court -- the second highest court in the land -- went even further in declaring arbitrators to be "sacred cows" and violence to be compatible with public policy.

In that most recent case, a Pennsylvania postal worker was upset because his supervisor, the local postmaster, had not promoted him as he had been promised. To show his displeasure, the employee fired two bullets through the windshield of the postmaster's car, damaging the windshield, dashboard and front seat. This constitutes a felony in almost every state in the nation, including Pennsylvania. Nonetheless, the arbitrator, relying upon the employee's prior unblemished thirteen-year record, held that there was not "good cause" to justify the employee's discharge and ordered his reinstatement. The Circuit Court (overruling the district court), basing its decision upon the Supreme Court's dictate that great deference be given to arbitrators, confirmed the arbitrator's action.

Only a few years back, both of these cases would have been described as mind boggling. Even today, most people are aghast that these cases could have been decided in the way they were. These results, however, reflect the great tolerance now afforded individuals in their conduct towards others generally in our society. This is especially true in the employment context, which but a short time ago had been blithely referred to as the master-servant relationship. This relationship is now on the cusp of having a state-enforced marriage status. Employees, only a few decades ago, had, lamentably, virtually no rights. No longer. Today their rights are formidable, their clout growing; legally, if not economically, they are in a privileged position.

In 1965, however, employee prerogatives were extremely limited. Certainly, McCoy's fighting words to his supervisor were then patently impermissible. True, "acceptable" language was in transition. But the revolution, while just around the corner, still had not arrived. The men then running American industry and presiding over society were the same men who had grown up or were already adults during the heyday of the movies -- that uniquely powerful manipulator of standards, conduct, and mores. Both Harden and McCoy, for example, were young and old enough to recall how, in order to get around the powerful barrier of censor Joseph Breen -- the most powerful mogul of them all -- and his Movie Production Code, the studio satraps, in their winning effort to permit Clark Gable to finish Margaret Mitchell's famous line, "Frankly, my dear..," the way she wrote it, had to fight like the dickens.

And later, in 1939, Harden and McCoy may have read and even chuckled about that colorful New York mayor, Fiorello LaGuardia, a "reform" minded liberal, who officially outlawed the word "burlesque" in advertisements and on marquees as being too risque. A few years later and a couple of hundred miles to the north, I recall that another charismatic mayor, Boston's inimitable James Michael Curley, a liberal rogue, closed down the play, "The Voice of the Turtle." Why? Because its star (Margaret Sullavan) said the word "hell" on stage in other than a biblical reference. There was no question, therefore, that McCoy, thirty some years ago, was not going to get away with insulting anyone, let alone his supervisor, with the "F" word. No way!

Prior to the hearing, Charles Harden, though no longer employed by Etiwanda Steel, agreed to testify and willingly confirmed the facts already noted. I put him on the stand as my one and only witness at the hearing. In his Southern drawl, he testified in a contrite but straightforward manner. He told of the preliminary verbal skirmishes that he and McCoy had engaged in that had brought about the altercation. The line of questioning then led to its planned culmination:

- Q. What did you do after he continued to ignore and walk away from you?

- A. I went up to him and told him to stop acting like a mouse and do a day's work.

- Q. What did the grievant do at that point?

- A. His face got red, he looked me straight in the eye and he yelled at me, "F--- you, you son of a bitch!"

(Transcripts in those days still showed a measure of modesty.)

Q. And what did you do then?

A. I smashed him in the jaw.

Self-satisfied, I then aimed to zip up the case, asking the final, seemingly superfluous question: "Why did you smack him?" expecting, naturally, that he would respond that he hit him because of McCoy's autogenesis suggestion. Harden instead answered, sternly, "Because he called me a son of a bitch."
It was "send-in-the-clowns" time.
The arbitrator, equally as surprised as I, gave me a knowing grin, as if to say, "Well, what are you going to do now, counsel?" We both realized my plight: my generation, more particularly, my milieu in my generation, had considered the four-letter word to be unmentionable. "Son-of-a-bitch", curiously perhaps, was generally considered nearly innocuous, more salty than salacious, hardly more rank than "son-of-a-gun." To rest my once ironclad case on the milquetoast "SOB" sobriquet -- without elucidation -- would invite defeat. Then, in a startling realization, it occurred to me that my witness was expressing a sentiment so dear and indigenous to those from the South -- pride in one's ancestry.
Desperately collecting my wits, and out of necessity daring to ask the next question, having been burned and bushwhacked by my star witness, I sought to turn my case around and came from the other direction:

Q. Why were you upset by his calling you a "son of a bitch?"

A. He had no cause to question my manhood and, for sure, nobody can insult my mother that way and expect to live.

Q. (now regaining a modicum of confidence) And were you upset by his epithet to you, that is, "F--- you"?

A. Absolutely not; that's physically impossible.

Mindful of Sir Walter Scott's hortation, "Charge, Chester, charge! On, Stanley, on!", I then "led" Harden to explain at length that such slurs on motherhood were not only "fighting words" back home in Alabama, but were used at one's great risk at Etiwanda, itself apparently a distant enclave of the South. In fact, Harden volunteered, to my delightful surprise, that except for the subject of women in general, the use of the "SOB" oath had brought on more fisticuffs over the years than anything else in the plant, where, it was plain, barnyard prose was everyman's art.

The arbitrator smiled as he saw me laboring to finesse a tour de force. My task and eventual victory, in retrospect, were made easier by Harden's obvious sincerity and deep conviction on the issue. Indeed, how else can such a powerful blow to a man's chin be explained? Fortunately, at no time during McCoy's testimony did he contradict or even question the seriousness of his ill-fated words directed toward Harden's maternity on that hot August day in front of the hearth.

*****

Those drawn or dragged to judicial turf are likely to be confounded by the added weight of cultural differences and communication difficulties. All those involved, the court itself included, carry their own cultural blinders or values. If these values are shared, then all participants are on the same level track; justice doesn't shoulder an added handicap. If the contestants reflect the same culture, but one different from the mullah, luck and artfulness come increasingly into play. (The constitutional safeguard of a jury of one's peers does not extend to judges.) If the judge's values, however, are akin to those of one party but not the other, the race seemingly is fixed from the start.

This dicey game has become especially pronounced and unsettling in recent years; this is particularly so in such burgeoning areas as California. Anglo-Saxon common law and legal institutions were developed in a homogeneous surrounding. Values were not only shared, they were embedded for ages. It is hard to imagine the genius of the common law being anything like that at all without an inherent commonality of the community. In our current society, however, the ties are often less than manufactured threads.

For almost three centuries, the culture of this society was, by and large, uniformly stamped, derived from common forebears, language, and institutions. Even throughout the nineteenth, and first half of the twentieth, century, the values of the predominant culture prevailed. The blending of new and different folk, while difficult and challenging, was, with one great exception (the Civil War), scarcely traumatic overall. Today, however, with the huge influx of peoples unfamiliar with our heritage, language and institutions, with the dramatic breakthrough of once ignored minorities into the equation of power, with the emergence of women as other than mates, with a bursting population, where, as in California, almost everyone recently came from somewhere else, with upheavals in stereotypical ways of life, and with the alacrity of events and invention, what remains shared is primarily television's wasteland, crowded freeways, and the religion of bowl games.

In such a free-for-all setting, the search for truth -- let alone justice -- is endless and elusive. Even according attorneys-en-large the best of purposes, the task of unearthing the truth and attaining substantial justice is not merely formidable, it appears overwhelming. Time and sweat alone cause such a burden on everyone involved that it can scarcely be borne by most. Lawyers are too expensive; the obscene cost of litigation, except in the simplest cases, leaves almost all but the affluent out in the cold;

overcrowded court calendars insure unending delay for the intrepid survivors. The limitation of human patience itself defies a meaningful probing of the nuances of polyglot tongues, the depths of complicated motives, the importance of variegated customs and the differences of human values -- without which justice is deaf.

Such a Casbahian cauldron invites, and is host to, exploitation. Thus, given this gruel, Thumb's Second Postulate, for example, really rises to the surface: "An easily understood, workable falsehood is more useful than a complex, incomprehensible truth."

Chapter 13.

Administration of the Law: Keeping Jeannie in the Bottle

Except for the combination of criminal and domestic relations law, most Americans come up against the legal process through what is known as Administrative Law. Regulatory bodies, governmental agencies, boards, commissions and authorities, particularly in the past half century and despite purported judicial safeguards, wield immense "administrative" power in our everyday lives, possibly affecting society as much as our court system. Generally more political than the courts, they are usually less responsible to their legislative overseers than is desirable or had been intended. At times, Administrative Law operates oblivious to checks and balances.

When the average citizen, resigned to the law's apparent indifference, shrugs and sighs, "Go fight City Hall," he also is expressing his own view as to who the real lawmakers are -- the bureaucrats who staff these government offices. He is not far wrong. The multitudinous alphabet agencies, mushrooming from the halls of administration at all levels of government, "make" more law than the framers of our Constitution ever envisioned; at times, they mock all three branches of government.

Most lawyers, always doing battle or brokering with powerdom, spend much of their time wrestling or shadow boxing with the likes of the Internal Revenue Service (IRS), Securities Exchange Commission (SEC), Public Utilities Commission (PUC), National Labor Relations Board (NLRB), Federal Communications Commission (FCC), Equal Employment Opportunity Commission (EEOC), Building and Safety Commission, state and local school boards, tax boards, harbor commissions, and the plethora of similarly powerful bureaus seemingly peopled by armies of anonymous autocrats. But these administrators and their minions are not automatons. They are a force with an agenda, sometimes following a blueprint drawn by the legislature, sometimes not.

Most employees in this phase of the legal process generally aim to administer and interpret the law as it was intended, or at least as it can be reasonably discerned. Frequently, however, like all staffs and attendants, they enlarge their own limited authority to the edge, and beyond the limits, of "colorable" license. They often legislate in mufti.

That this pleonexia -- power playing -- is not simply an individual propensity but a group fixation was illustrated to me in the early 1970s. An important client and friend of mine asked me to "represent" his company before the Workers' Compensation Board; he felt that his insurance carrier and its attorneys were not protecting his interests or seeking justice. One of his employees, a man who had worked for him for twenty years through life's trials and tribulations, yearned for retirement. The only way that would be possible at age 60 was by his getting a medical workers' compensation award by feigning a heart condition, allegedly induced by the asserted conduct of my admittedly excitable though highly intelligent client. The employee confessed his stratagem to my client and asked his acquiescence in this ploy; after all, it would cost my client hardly anything, at most a minor increase in his workers' compensation rates.

My client, having literally dug himself out of a Nazi extermination camp and striven to make his success in this country, was not about to become a patsy to such conduct. Thus, his exhortation to me: "Put some backbone in the lawyer for the insurance carrier; fight!"

When I arrived at the Workers' Compensation Board hearing room, crowded with litigants and all types of counsel, it had the appearance of a poor man's stock market trading floor. After ferreting out the attorney for the insurance company, I was astonished to learn that she felt that there was little point in putting up too vigorous a case. The way things were handled there, she explained, was to see to it that the claimants received meaningful compensation, regardless of the merits of their claims.

"Why?" I exclaimed. I was told frankly by this attorney, who was supposed to be defending the rights of her principal -- the employer, my client -- that in this arena, all involved considered that they were performing a social service. These people, she said, referring generally to all similar claimants seeking succor, had to be taken care of in some fashion by someone, now or some time soon, and it was just as well that workers' compensation provide the societal relief necessary as some other branch of society.

I knew that workers' compensation legislation had not been enacted with this purpose in mind. I doubt that, even now, any legislature would acquiesce in this philosophy. Though I was successful in stymieing this particular freeloading adventure, the weltanschauung that invites such self-aggrandizement has clearly been administratively engrafted into the process.

This universal ego trip -- often, and at times correctly, described as compassion -- reached its apogee in the civil rights movement of the Sixties. Few can seriously question the need and legal justification for much, if not most, of the civil rights legislation passed during that period. The inequities of our complacent society prior to that time were so manifest that a revolution was required, even if in its wake serious injustices were inflicted upon the innocent. Still, some of the excesses were not only unnecessary and inane, but counterproductive and, at times, comical.

Aside from leaders who have involved us in wars or in great epics, two people who had a most profound effect on this society in the last fifty years are hardly identifiable by the average American. The first was the little known and hardly remembered Beardsley Ruml (a middle-echelon bureaucrat), the man who devised the "pay as you go" tax program initiated during World War II. He and his "wartime measure" have been responsible, from a political feasibility perspective, for paving the way for much of the costly social welfare and defense programs that the federal government has spawned since. Without this "easy" withholding method of paying taxes, the populace would hardly have acquiesced in such burdensome expenditures. Indeed, then Governor Ronald Reagan in 1967 declared that his "feet were in concrete" on the withholding issue -- he was adamantly against it. He wisely perceived that without withholding in California, he could indirectly but effectively block social programs he philosophically opposed. Only after years of rough political battle and millions lost in revenue did Reagan yield and allow tax withholding. In so capitulating, Reagan, for better or worse, lost a Big One.

The second near-forgotten giant-mover was a most charming and intelligent legislator, Senator Margaret Chase Smith of Maine. This shrewd and courageous woman -- also one of the first in Congress to stand up to Senator Joe McCarthy -- asserted on the Senate floor during the debates on civil rights legislation initiating the Equal Employment Opportunity Act that she had a "non-controversial" amendment to add to the pending bills aimed to safeguard primarily the economic welfare of Negroes. This amendment simply added women to those groups needing further protection. Little did many of her colleagues realize that within 25 years, this innocuous amendment would come to be the prime concern of those administering civil rights statutes. Since 1971, the Supreme Court, itself, has heard over a score of sex-discrimination controversies. This is an exceptionally high number of cases accepted by the Court, perhaps surpassing those in any other controversial category.

By the middle 1960's, the metes and bounds of that newly enacted legislation were still indeterminate. Most of the battles were to be fought in the courts, but one early casualty of this anti-discriminatory legislation was the free press -- in particular, the then usual and acceptable manner by which employers advertised and newspapers printed "Help Wanted" ads. Virtually all printed media published such advertisements by dividing employment opportunities available into "Help Wanted - Male" and "Help Wanted - Female" categories. The Equal Employment Opportunity Commission was determined to end this practice, seemingly an invidious form of sexual discrimination. Accordingly, it barred the use of this time-honored habit and ruled it a prima facie violation of these federal statutes.

Hollie's Hardware, a company with numerous retail stores, employed a female supervisor who had, for a quarter century, reigned over the accounting department with an iron fist covered with but a veneer of velvet, performing her duties in a manner that brooked interference from none. All 25 women under Jean Mann and all executives over her appeared to kowtow, even quake, in the face of her crisp efficiency and razor-sharp knowledge. Her distaff assistants, however, did not often stay the course -- for obvious reasons. The company found itself again and again in the position of having to advertise for a new assistant to this forewoman fatale.

Thus, in 1966, once again, it placed a newspaper ad under the "Help Wanted - Female" classification. Numerous jobseekers applied for this attractive-sounding position. Two of the applications, however, were submitted by men, undaunted by, or oblivious to, the sex criterion. The company replied in writing to those two applicants that it was not considering male applicants, diplomatically noting "because of the nature of the job." Meaning, of course, that the company harbored doubts as to whether any man in his right mind would or could work for this female behemoth. Besides, all the other employees in the department were women and there was no toilet for a man, although this was not so stated.

One of these male applicants knew his rights, and he was not going to put up with this "obvious" reverse discrimination, even if he could not get the officials of any embryonic feminist group to support him in his crusade. He immediately fired off a charge to the EEOC, demanding that his rights be upheld and that he be given the job in question or damages therefor. The EEOC, initially in blushing bride fashion, did enter the fray, however unaccustomed it was to taking up the cudgels on behalf of a Waspman. But the agency had to contend with the principle and, as I would discover, it developed its own agenda and soon pursued it, no holds barred.

Representing the company, I was quickly served with hefty documents demanding, among other things, that I supply data on the sex and racial backgrounds of all of the company's numerous and far-flung employees. Up to that time, most specialists in this area of the law, myself included, had thought that the obtaining of such information was clearly taboo. Yes, in most instances, obtaining such information was absolutely forbidden, except one must absolutely provide it when the EEOC asks for it. At least that was the status of the law at that time. I was then asked to provide the EEOC with a full breakdown of the racial composition of the community where the company's offices were located. Lastly, in order to settle the case, the administrators of the EEOC would require that Hollie's agree to adopt a formal affirmative action program whereby it would hire over a period of years certain numbers of blacks, Mexican-Americans, Asian-Americans, and original Americans (nothing was said about women, since most of the office and clerical employees were women!). But the avalanche of EEOC demands had nothing to do with sex bias and were aimed to relieve problems that the charge of reverse discrimination against a man had not even raised and that did not really exist in this company.

Indignantly, I informed my law school classmate, who was now in charge of the local EEOC, that I had no intention whatsoever of complying with such a far-reaching and overreaching demand. I simply advised her to "do what she had to do," "take her best shot;" I would "see her in court." Though it was not my intention to make my client the vehicle for bringing the issue before the federal courts, I was determined not to allow what I considered to be a gross misuse of legislative power by the bureaucracy, whatever good intentions might lie beneath the surface. My client fully backed me up. Indeed, I have no doubt that, based upon the EEOC's audacious action in the matter and its reaction to this fiat, my client was prepared not only to take on the entire Great Society, but most of the New Deal and Fair Deal as well!

The next move was up to the EEOC, and I awaited it. Considerable time went by, however, and nothing happened. The EEOC did not bring up the complaint that it had threatened. More than six months later, I chanced to meet my EEOC friend and inquired about the delay. She said they were still working on it. When almost a year had gone by, I went out of my way to ascertain what was happening. Then I learned that the EEOC was planning to dismiss the charge.

Delighted with this news, I was also curious as to what had prompted the bureaucracy to backtrack and to cease pillorying my client for seemingly discriminating in favor of women. This was one of the very first reverse discrimination cases to surface after the passage of the 1964 Act. The EEOC had given every indication that this was to be a showcase effort on its part, to highlight that the Commission could be as vigorous on behalf of men as women. This "fairness," to my mind, was reminiscent of

Anatole France's pithy observation that "The law, in its majestic equality, forbids the rich as well as the poor to sleep under the bridges." But now the EEOC had fled the field of battle, swordside. Why, I asked my law school "buddy." She told me, in whispers.

It seems, she confided, that at the time the EEOC made its demands on my client, it perfunctorily sent a copy of its proposals to the charging party, the man on whose behalf it was supposedly acting. When he read that the EEOC was seeking to require my client to adopt a far-reaching affirmative action program for the benefit of blacks, Hispanics and other minority groups, he was greatly upset. But not for my reasons. Spurning a compromise that would have required Hollie's to hire him for its next accounting department opening, he bluntly denounced the proposed affirmative action, or quasi-quota, program. The bottom line, as he told the EEOC, was that he was "not going to be part of any deal that helps niggers to become employed!!"

Given his inimitable stance and view of the 1964 legislation, the EEOC quietly abandoned his cause; in fact, it never formally advised me or my client of its disposition of the case. Justly, it was unceremoniously buried. Ironically, from a narrow legal point of view, this mean-spirited citizen did have a "colorable" right that was being infringed, the likes of Jean Mann notwithstanding. But there can be little question that Congress in 1964 hardly had in mind upholding such "rights," even if they benefited men without such Jim Crow sentiments.

That the zealous interpretation of laws can lead to unjust -- often weird -- results should no longer surprise us. This truism, however, is nowhere more manifest than in the anti-discrimination field. The interpretation given to much of this legislation has made the law itself a laughingstock. In 1987, I came across another such example of the consequences of an unbridled interpretation of Title VII of the Civil Rights Act. In a case that could hardly have been envisioned by Congress in 1964, a federal district court judge held that a fiercely religious sect must hire a woman bus driver to serve its all-male religious school -- the United Talmudic Academy, a private institution founded and run by Hasidic Jews of the Satmir sect. Aside from the fact that such a hiring would jeopardize the driver's safety (since the sect had <u>deeply</u>, near fanatically, held religious and emotional beliefs as to the separation of the sexes in many day to day activities), the court's position not only went beyond legislative intent, it portended a serious infringement on the First Amendment. Could the same court require the Hasidic congregation to integrate the temple, that is, enjoin the segregation of men and women in the synagogue? Hardly, but the issue is essentially the same.

In the very same month that the epic Civil Right Act of 1964 was signed by Lyndon Johnson, paradoxically, presidential contender Barry Goldwater, who unequivocally denounced the legislation, enunciated the polemic proposition that "Extremism in the defense of liberty is no vice; moderation in the pursuit of justice is no virtue." As rhetoric, it is rousing. From experience, it almost always is destined to be disillusioning. At times, however, such a <u>cri</u> <u>de</u> <u>coeur</u> is necessary in order to retain a measure of liberty, achieve a modicum of justice, and uplift the human spirit.

Chapter 14.

The Counselor: Lettuce, Sit Down, and Reason Together

As the layman is likely to be surprised by the far-reaching power of legal bureaucracy, he also probably has a television reception, channel vision, of what lawyers actually do. What and where does the attorney "practice"? Despite the popular image to the contrary and the bursting calendars of criminal courts, only a fraction of those who pass the bar ever do more than a piddling amount of criminal work; most lawyers could not handle even their own traffic citation cases. In fact, the majority of attorneys do not do trial work. They are more likely to be "solicitors," in the English manner; that is, they handle matters that are not in litigation or they prepare but do not try cases; barristers do the court work (and get the "glory"). Even the most accomplished trial attorney rarely spends more than a few months annually in the courtroom. More than 90% of legal controversies are, fortunately, settled.

The greater part of most attorneys' work, furthermore, does not even directly relate to litigation. Indeed, much of their time and advice are spent on either nonlegal or nonpaying concerns. But this, too, is lawyering, for the lawyer is primarily a counselor.

The crux of the attorney's work is to predict. From such predictions, plans of action (or inaction) are devised. The attorney counsels whether the application of a given set of facts will lead to the enforcement of an existing law. He also advises whether that rule will still be viable in the foreseeable future, because "The Law" itself is always in transition. This is a delicate task. Trying to predict and shape your client's future based upon the ambiguities of past case law and existing statutes that will often be addressed by trial judges less knowledgeable on the point than anyone else involved in the case is difficult enough; but speculating as to which party's testimony will be most credible, and then divining what an appellate court will do if the case "goes up," insures ever increasing sales of Maalox.

My participation in the heady lettuce fuss and labor strife of the early 1970's underscored for me that crystal balls can turn to bubbles and that lawyers must consider that a favorable ruling interpreting the law today may well be passe tomorrow.

Cesar Chavez, a charismatic and sincere leader for a cause, after years of pyrrhic skirmishing, with his movement and his United Farm Workers following it to the Rubicon, crossed over into open warfare not only against belligerent farm owners, but the competitive Teamsters Union. The liberal establishment and the Catholic Church, a unique coupling, crusaded to organize the largely itinerant and disadvantaged farm workers.

From his base of operations in Delano, in Steinbeck's own San Joaquin Valley, he issued his clarion marching orders: take on the supermarkets, do battle with the chains, force the sale of lettuce picked only by members of the UFW, inveigh the consumer to spurn Teamster-handled lettuce.

My client, Nelson's Market, a highly successful "Mom and Pop" produce store in Escondido (near San Diego), found itself in the center of this battlefield, a victim of the internecine clash between these two warring and strangely different "labor organizations." On Nelson's land, the modern battle of Antietam began to rage. Squads of pickets carrying placards stormed and surrounded the market, interfering with the ability of customers to enter or leave the store. Their picket signs urged that the public not buy "scab" lettuce; ironically, lettuce picked by hands tainted by Teamsters membership. Soon the siege of the store took on a more militant character. Dozens of UFW protesters simply engaged in a concerted sit-down at the store's entrance. If a venturesome customer sought to infiltrate this Mexican-style Maginot line, he was likely to be the butt of hurled epithets, such as "perujo" -- south of the border for "queer."

All this in the Yuletide season of 1970. Indeed, within days of Christmas the picketing took on a religious intensity seldom witnessed in this country. To bolster the flagging spirits of the picketers and to further cordon off access to the market, Father Victor Salendini, an intrepid leader of the movement, surrounded by Mexican and "Blue Eagle" flags (the symbol of the UFW), conducted an honest-to-God Mass in Nelson's parking lot. Surely, one witnessing this dedicated priest reading psalms and singing the Lord's praises in the midst of this supermarket war zone might well have had the eerie feeling that he was at the gates of Armageddon.

The elderly Nelsons, peering glumly out of their near empty market, were unmoved. Then, in the St. Nick of time, I got a call to arms from the besieged. In a matter of hours, having been summoned to the field of battle, I surveyed the situation and prepared a counterattack. There was no question about it. Chavez and the Lord's emissary, whatever their motives, were engaged in unlawful jurisdictional and massive picketing in violation of California law. And Cesar would have to yield up to the state, then governed by Ronald Reagan. I aimed to enforce that law and enjoin Chavez, Salendini and Company.

The injunctive relief I sought was, I think, unique. First, I argued that the picketing should be stopped because it was jurisdictional in purpose. On this ground the existing California statute prohibited any picketing; the court agreed, and upheld my position. My second argument was that massive picketing, interfering with customer traffic, traditionally is prohibited. When the court granted my prayer for an injunction on this additional basis, however it was, in effect, acknowledging as an historical first, that "Mass" picketing -- literally -- may also be prohibited.

The restraining order was quite a Christmas gift to the Nelsons. Chavez' "La Causa" was dealt a crushing defeat; his movement was cut down at San Diego's Palomar mountain pass. Its "causa" (legal case), moreover, was just about over. Or was it?

A few days after my clients had enjoyed their holiday repast, I met with them and advised them that we should compromise our victory and make a deal with the UFW that would allow the union to engage in a very limited amount of picketing, say two or three pickets in toto, provided that their signs were truthful and their conduct orderly. The Nelsons were confused and surprised by this advice. They imagined that the holiday spirit had gone to my head. Why such magnanimity, they asked. "We won; the law's on our side. Why give them anything?"

It's true, I answered. The California Jurisdictional Strike Act, which had existed on the books and been sustained by the courts for decades, did support our all-out position. But the UFW was prepared to appeal this case, as well as others of a similar nature, I informed them, and given the composition of the state and federal courts, I was convinced that our victory would not be upheld on appeal. The rulings in our favor in this and prior cases were constitutionally shaky, in part because the California statute may have interfered with federal law, but primarily because it may have unduly undermined free speech rights under the First Amendment. Such were the winds of the times.

This explanation was undoubtedly gibberish to the Nelsons, but when I assured them that such a settlement would make innocuous whatever little picketing we would permit and that after a couple of weeks even those pickets would likely go away voluntarily, they reluctantly reconciled themselves to my advice. When I further noted that such a compromise by us would spare them further attorney's fees, they greeted and grasped the settlement with enthusiasm.

And so it came to pass. Within days, the limited picketing proved barely an irritant. Within a week, the last of Cesar's rear guard troops left Nelson's field, transferred to duty elsewhere. Less than four months afterwards the California Supreme Court, in another case of the very same nature arising in Northern California, upheld Chavez and the UFW's contention that the California statute must yield to the dictates of the free speech guarantee of the Constitution. The Court allowed picketing of the type that was the basis of the Nelson settlement, though the Court has never to this day specifically given its blessings or imprimatur to enjoining Mass picketing.

* * * * *

That the settlement, which was fully just to my client, also coincided with my own view of fairness and the Constitution was fortunate; that it satisfied the needs and those of the larger community was no less important....

* * * * *

Chapter 15.

... Beyond Winning ...
Vince Lombardi and Joe Kennedy Were Wrong

The role of the attorney is not fulfilled by his professional caring for his clients. His duty, or at least the need for him, extends beyond the confines of his own practice. His professional constituency encompasses the broader community and, ideally, that community has some claim to the talents he hones. There is an unwritten pact that lawyers "owe" the community more than others -- tradesmen, guilds, or even other professions.

Despite the recent weakening of this largely unconscious covenant, lawyers, for a variety of reasons, continue to share their skills in major ways beyond their own professional practices. The significant amount of pro bono work performed by thousands of attorneys -- while plainly far less than should be forthcoming -- is an immediate example of the paid-in-part debt attorneys offer the community. Organized bar activities frequently are directly aimed at alleviating society's ills, including trying to make the judicial process meaningful and just to citizens other than the affluent and powerful.

The lawyer's social writ is <u>en large</u>. It extends outside the courthouse, away from his office, beyond his 1040, line 30 (Adjusted Gross Income). The orbit of his presence remains impressive: lawyers dominate most legislative bodies throughout the country and, of course, have a virtual monopoly on the judiciary. They are usually in the forefront of citizens' groups, support organizations, and community activity in general. They are predominant in the leadership of both public bureaucracies and private associations that serve vital social purposes. In almost all such activities, their skills and methods are especially important to the success of the endeavor. Even in those instances when it is both possible and advantageous that "The Law" be excluded from the process, the lawyer's traits and training are welcomed assets for resolving problems. Their ability to reconcile and organize people, facts and ideas is prized. They cement society.

The ubiquitous problem-solver. Thus far in my career, I have not met my personally imposed "quota." The reasons (or rationalizations) are for the moment unimportant. But one such problem-solving task that occupied my attention -- and which exemplifies the lawyer's role in the larger community -- came about as an outgrowth of the Watts race riots in Los Angeles in 1965.

The social revolution of the Sixties reached a physical and psychological crest in the Watts riots. This terrifying trauma tore the placid cover of passivity from the Southern California landscape. Shattered, perhaps forever, was the satisfying assuredness that Los Angeles's genteel climate and California's economic cornucopia precluded the intrusion of the ghetto and its explosiveness. After five August days of relentless carnage, with dozens dead in its wake and hundreds of millions of dollars of property destroyed by those most in need of it, the stunned Establishment awoke from its indifference. Within days, the community, in search of answers to "why" and methods as to "how," sprung to activity.

Among myriad efforts to alleviate the conditions that lent thrust to the conflagration, various committees and study groups came into being -- as if spontaneously -- to deal with its various components. I accepted a position on a subcommittee analyzing "Employment Opportunities in the Minority Community." Essentially, our duty was to address the staggering unemployment plight of blacks. Such an assignment, delegated to a three-man lay committee, was as presumptuous as it was implausible. That did not make the effort any less necessary.

All three of us were lawyers. There, any commonality ended, save for our sincerity in wanting to make a positive contribution. Our approaches would prove to be as different as our backgrounds. I was designated chairman, apparently on the assumption that, being a management attorney in labor relations with a reputation of still retaining liberal political tendencies, I could bring to the assignment bridgework.

This very combination of factors, however, undoubtedly did not set well with my counterpart, John Reed Black. He was an older attorney who had a well-deserved reputation as a brilliant advocate. Not incongruously, he was equally renowned for his radical political views, though he always acted within the law and with obvious professionalism. While he may have shunned stridency, liberals of any stripe did not escape his scorn; in fact, in concert with a long-recognized phenomenon, liberals were the real enemies of the far left. Entre nous -- alone -- there was, therefore, bound to be, if nothing else, a showdown or a good show. There was both.

Roosevelt White, in the final analysis, gave the Committee potential clout -- or at least acceptability. Not yet thirty, he had been practicing hardly more than a year. Despite his self-acknowledged inexperience, both in the law and in the nature of the work before us, he brought added intelligence and earnestness to our task. His being black gave a different and needed dimension -- as well as an ecumenical hue -- to our charge. Most appropriately, the direction he would eventually take would likely decide the Committee's course. After all, White and blacks was what it was all about.

Or was it? After but two sessions, the critical issue before us became starkly focused. We were at the threshold of the great national debate that was just beginning to foment with the advent of the Civil Rights Act of 1964 and the implementation of the Great Society. It rages today; it promises to explode tomorrow; it is almost certain to be with us forever. In a pluralistic democracy that tends to preach egalitarianism and meritocracy at the same time, how can economic security be assured for all when, as added obstacles, an historical yoke (slavery) and a human hangup (discrimination) combine to make the terrain even rougher than it would otherwise be?

From out of this dilemma comes the concept of quotas. That is what soon confronted our Committee as the core of its consideration. But as the courts and the country have come to be acutely aware, especially in the past quarter century, the imposition of quotas (or their equivalent, under different nomenclature) creates a conundrum that cuts across the Constitution. Quotas, when effectuated to favor one race or sex at the expense of another and to cause not merely offense, but harm, to that other, are, when in the public domain, patently anathema to both our Constitution and ethos. They are, in a word, unjust. The absence of quotas, however, often allows the consequences of prior discrimination to go uncorrected, thereby causing or insuring the continual advantage of one race or sex at the expense of the other. It is, equally, constitutionally unacceptable. To permit such an injustice by inaction is to cause it. If we accept the further proposition that all that is legal is not moral and all that is immoral is not illegal, then the anomaly is inescapable: quotas (or their equivalent), or the absence of quotas in many circumstances, are each immoral.

Like the Three Wise Men of Gotham, the Committee initially drifted in this painful puzzlement. John Black soon changed that; he gave direction in no uncertain terms. He proposed that the Committee recommend that both the federal and state government step in and order an unprecedented redistribution of employment opportunities not only in Watts, but throughout Southern California. He poignantly cited the dire unemployment statistics in Watts and other black sections of Los Angeles County -- ranging from 20 to 40 percent. He pointed out the underemployment among the men in these areas and the bleak outlook in their non-fortunes. He proposed, in some detail, a remedy that essentially would require all employers -- from smokestacked factories to university faculties -- to hire blacks at a two-to-one ratio over other races until black unemployment was no higher than caucasian. And there was to be no question about qualifications; employers were to train the unqualified. His plan, to describe it in a nutshell, was a class act.

Rosie White was deeply moved by Black's presentation. He turned to me for concurrence. Uneasily but unequivocally, I took off against the quota program Black had espoused. I pointed out its historical bigoted birth, its discriminatory implications, and its self-defeating goals. I argued that rather than exalt the black worker, it would demean him. I deplored the constitutional consequences of such colorization of constitutional rights. But, hesitantly, I confessed the moral dilemma.

Black scorned what he labeled my overly pedantic approach. At the same time, he scoffed at what he called my "pretentious" concern as to the moral ambiguities of the problem. He sneered at my "warmed over" suggestion that we urge a redoubled effort at developing training programs. He declaimed that such programs merely trained a perpetual proletariat. Besides, he argued, what good is training, if blacks are the last hired and the first fired? He took me on in a dialectic mode, where he clearly excelled. My weakness, however, was not his skill but my lack of a meaningful alternative. Realizing this, I sought a delay, another meeting, before acting on Black's proposal. Thus far, sitting down and reasoning together had not gone in the direction I had envisioned. Rosie, who seemed genuinely fascinated by the verbal sorties buzzing around him and who also harbored some unsettling doubts about Black's dramatic program, welcomed the opportunity for a week's recess to think the whole thing over.

How to solve the problem of the moral dilemma posed by quotas was my dilemma. Only faintly conscious that this intractable enigma would possess the three branches of government for generations to come, I ventured for a solution. Well, not necessarily a solution, for such matters are seldom solved. But, hopefully, a reconciliation or at least a temporary resolution. And I employed a lawyer's tools: empiricism, elimination, and imagination. The "trick" was to use the Constitution itself to supply the means to create a program -- not merely a policy -- to accomplish economic gain for a certain group without running afoul of the constitutional rights of other groups. The more I thought about it, the clearer it became that this very type of problem weighed heavily upon the New Deal in the constitutional crisis thirty years before; the tactical ways of coping could be used again.

During the week before our next committee meeting, I slowly pulled together the pieces. First, like most of the New Deal programs, my proposal rested upon the Commerce Clause of the Constitution. The heavy and disproportionate level of unemployment in certain geographic areas was a burden upon, and interfered with, interstate commerce. That these areas were primarily black was, legally speaking, incidental. Secondly, the government had the right to alleviate this burden, particularly since it was interfering with the National Defense. The end, therefore, was constitutionally sanctioned; the means need only not be prohibited.

Step Three "simply" authorized the legislature to take the latest census tract and superimpose it on the Bureau of Labor Statistics' monthly computation depicting the unemployment figures in the Southern California counties. Lastly, employers, or at least those engaged in national defense work or supported by government expenditures, were to be directed to hire new employees from those areas shown to have the highest unemployment until such time as the ratio of the jobless in such geographic areas was reduced to near the level of that existing throughout all of Southern California. Nothing in this entire proposed legislation mentioned or referred to race. Quotas were to be based solely on the unemployed, whoever and wherever they might be. That the program accomplished the result we were seeking -- drastically reducing black joblessness -- without undermining constitutional principles, would be readily acknowledged. If it had the added and winsome effect of causing some unemployed whites to move into black neighborhoods so as to better enable them to obtain employment -- and coincidentally alleviate to some degree the segregated housing problem, sort of gilding the lily -- so much the better. All lawyer-like.

Having armed myself with this written proposal, I called together the Committee. Black arrived, confident that his own iron-ringed proposal would now be supported by Rosie. When Rosie White mentioned that he had consulted with his constituency, I gleaned that I had my work cut out for me that evening. After J.R. Black asked that his proposal be adopted and sent to the parent committee, I took out my proposal, gave them copies, and explained it step-by-step. When I had finished, Black took the offensive. After some preliminary remarks relating to his desire to tear off my liberal mask with the expectation of finding nothing more than the typical management-attorney reactionary, he went to the merits of my proposal. He resented my program because he felt it was too clever by half, a namby-pamby scheme to avoid the surgery to the corpus politic that he felt was long overdue.

I didn't especially resent his barbs until he went beyond simply implying that this "scheme" of mine lacked solid legal foundation. That blow to the solar plexus opened up an hour-long, provocative but scholarly discourse between J.R. and me. It was played out, except for the mutually rude interruptions, as though each of us were arguing before the Supreme Court (where he had repeatedly shone, and I, the year before on my maiden trip, had gone down, eight-zip).

All the time that this lively show was going on, our audience, Rosie White, seemingly spellbound, was the real object of the engagement. We were his suitors. Had Rosie not been so engrossed and less dedicated, he would have savored the irony of these two honkies fighting over who was the staunchest supporter of his rights. We were as solicitous to him as though we were superpowers, angling for the heart and mind of the Third World; in this case, we anxiously catered to and awaited "Rosie's Outlook."

A Minority of One

Rosie White was in a bind. He was both a lawyer and a black. He had many cherished constituencies and therefore likely more than one conscience. Listening to J.R. and me, you could visually follow him lean one way, then the other, back again and forth again. He was indeed finding himself in the predicament of the all-too-human rabbi. For years the rabbi's wife witnessed him in their home trying to advise and resolve the many disputes of his shetl's congregation. He almost universally gave the same judgment. Thus, during one such wrangling the rabbi heard a husband bemoan his wife's conduct. The rabbi told him he was right. Later, he separately heard the wife's grievances on the same subject. When she finished, he said to her, "You're right." The rabbi's wife had viewed this scenario too often. She soon berated him for his hypocrisy.

"First you tell the husband he is right. Then you tell the wife she is right. How can they both be right? <u>You</u> are a meshugginah!" she cried out.

"You, too, are right," the rabbi sighed.

But White could not take sanctuary by this escape route. He was no rabbi. He was a committeeman whose decisive vote was awaited. And he cast his lot with Black. Democracy and its majority had spoken. But the "rules" allowed the minority to speak out, and I attached my written minority report to the Black and White document that was forwarded to the parent committee. There, both reports languished. I had, from the start, suspected such a denouement. After all, most study papers, including heavily financed governmental ones, seldom make it out of the library's subterranean stacks; they come to rest in the silence of the archives. Indeed, little was ever heard again about any of the Watts-inspired group activity. Vietnam, Watergate, and busing occupied the public's forum when football, baseball and basketball didn't.

Still, the dialogue itself was and remains important. We should not be too cynical about such efforts. First, because such dialogue is essential to democracy and to the human psyche. Moreover, it stirs ideas that have a strange way of rising, Phoenix-like, well after the burning is over and the burned out have left the scene of battle. The search for justice is timeless as well as endless.[9]

---

[9] In June 1995, thirty years after Watts (and almost ten years after the foregoing Chapter was originally written), the Supreme Court in Adarand Construction, Inc., greatly restricted government's right to engage in affirmative action programs that gave racial preference in contracting of work. The following month President Clinton, as he previously requested, received a Justice Department report on affirmative action. That report and subsequent Department action sparked plans for a new type of affirmative action -- bottomed upon the concept of "place, not race."

Chapter 16.

Justice -- More or Less

Any search for justice surely leads to the resigned conclusion that it seldom can be obtained quickly or cheaply. Justice is a hard, often tortuous odyssey, not a serene summer cruise. The effort is further encumbered by an inherent jigsaw puzzle within the judicial system. Each tribunal that is a piece of the process has its own row to hoe, its own, often fixed, role; even its own values. Thus, the interpretation of "justice" is frequently different at each station along the way; it has a Rashomon-like quality.

Justice has conflicting meanings to dissimilar trial judges, be they a Wyzanski, a Wright, or a Clarke. The appellate court, in turn, has a different perspective on the case before it than the trier of fact. Law -- presumptively pristine -- supposedly emerges at the higher stratospheres. It frequently does so, however, at the expense of garden variety, or "grassroots" justice. This "higher" law, moreover, is often fickle: when it is obtuse and ambiguous, it has amazing longevity; when it is simple and precise, it is likely to be transitory.

The story is often told about Judge Holmes' cryptic view of his role on the Supreme Court. The main storyteller was Judge Charles Wyzanski, Jr., who often related how Holmes, then age 90, was having a conversation with the great Judge Learned Hand while they were walking together toward the Supreme Court building. When they reached the courthouse, Holmes bid his friend Hand goodbye and began to climb the stairs. Waving farewell, Hand called out to Holmes, "Go forth and do justice." Holmes continued to climb the stairs, then stopped, turned around and hastened back, caught up with Hand and breathlessly said to him, "Sir, I go forth to enforce the law, not to do justice." This story has been repeated for over sixty-five years, to nail down the point that appellate courts, and by implication, all courts, are devoted to the task of interpreting and enforcing the law, not in seeking to impose justice. Holmes was an exemplar of that school of judicial philosophy, one shared by a number of leading scholars and learned judges.

That Holmesian stance, I submit, cannot be taken too literally. If those on the Supreme Court cannot be part of the process that produces justice, who can? Even if there is a difference in approach between an activist and a non-activist judge, each creates law and embodies justice by weighing facts, interpreting often ambiguous statutes, and applying or distinguishing murky precedents. The end result is labeled "law." This, avowedly, may not equate with justice. But no thinking person can assert that there is a clear-cut distinction between them, or deny the overlapping aim of these two concepts. Surely, the legislature does not insure justice, although it may strive for it. Its enactments usually must be general to be efficacious. The amalgam in each case is for courts to determine, and therein lies the possibility of institutional justice.

This anomaly often places all judges in a position of uncertainty, making their role the most difficult to define, which is the hallmark of the "least dangerous branch." But if the judicial duality of purpose often poses a dilemma, its importance is critical. For you can have justice without law; and you can have law without justice. But, neither condition can last for long.

Two of my early cases highlight this variation on the theme of lawful justice. Both deal more with concepts than with people, more with heavy law than with light laughter. We were not promised a rose garden along the eternal gray brick road on the search for justice. That concept is hard work just to understand, let alone to apply. What we may learn, however, is likely to be most lasting.

The facts in the first of these cases (each in the early 1960s), Thriftimart v. Retail Clerks, were relatively simple. Thriftimart, a major supermarket chain in California and a member of a multi-employer association, had a collective bargaining agreement with the Retail Clerks Union. In the late 1950s, Thriftimart purchased the stock of a discount store operation, then quite different from a supermarket. This operation, called "MORE," was composed of five discount centers.

Prior to the sale, the Retail Clerks had tried to organize the MORE stores, but the employees formally rejected the union. Then, after Thriftimart bought these MORE stores and continued them as a separate operation and subsidiary, the union demanded that Thriftimart force these employees to be bound to the same agreement that covered the Thriftimart employees, Thriftimart (and MORE) naturally rejected that demand. The union then ignored the MORE officials and demanded that Thriftimart itself litigate that issue in accordance with the arbitration provisions of the existing Union-Thriftimart collective bargaining agreement.

Just prior to that time, the Supreme Court had rendered a trio of decisions significantly expanding the scope and importance of the arbitration process in labor relations. Indeed, from that time on, as discussed in Chapters 8 and 9, there have come to be very few limits to the reach of arbitration in labor relations disputes. The power of private arbitrators is now clearly greater than that of federal and state court judges. This, in itself, is a reflection of the inherent power of Judges not only to expand or limit their own authority, but to fashion powerful new legal forums that may be responsible to no one.

Thriftimart agreed to go to arbitration confident that the dean of a well-known law school, having been selected by the parties as the arbitrator (approximately one-third of the faculty professors of major law schools frequently arbitrate both public and private disputes), would rule in the supermarket's favor. The union recognized that its case was weak, since MORE and Thriftimart were entirely separate entities. Discount store operations had just begun to spring up on a chainwide basis and were patently different from the typical supermarket. The union expected to lose, but it took its "best shot" (in labor law parlance).

The dean, who had done a considerable amount of arbitrating, was then being seriously considered for an appointment to the California appellate court. His subsequent ruling in the matter (since it was favorable to his political supporters) did not hinder his possible selection, an appointment which came within a few months after this decision. He held that Thriftimart must put the employees of MORE under the collective bargaining agreement to which Thriftimart was a party. None of the employees of MORE had ever voted for the union. Indeed, they had voted against it. Neither the employees nor MORE itself had participated in the arbitration. They had not even been invited to attend. And neither MORE nor its employees even knew about the arbitration until the arbitrator had rendered his award. It was at this point that MORE asked me to represent it.

The questions this case posed seemed obvious: Was the award valid and binding? Or did it fall below the "Plimsoll line" of fairness? Did the arbitrator even have jurisdiction? Could his decision be overturned?

Having then been in practice only a few years, I had little doubt that I had the answers to these questions. Obviously, the arbitrator was wrong. Patently, he could not give such a decision and, clearly, he had no jurisdiction. So cocksure was I that, for the first (and last) time, I guaranteed my client that we would prevail.

On behalf of MORE, I immediately intervened in the action in the Superior Court in Los Angeles which the union had brought to affirm the arbitrator's award. The court, significantly, allowed me to intervene, but went on from there to hold against MORE on the ultimate question. That court, to my surprise, ruled that because of the "great deference that is to be given to arbitration," it would not set aside the award. In effect, the judge gave sober deference to my cogent arguments and with no less deference rejected them. He sent me on my way, epigrammatically announcing, "I may be in error, but I am not in doubt!"

I was but mildly daunted; I had other avenues available in the pursuit of justice, I could either appeal that state court judgment or seek in the federal district court to have the judgment set aside as being repugnant to federal law and the Constitution. I chose the latter course. In this, I was joined by very competent counsel for Thriftimart. I filed papers in the federal court seeking to set aside the arbitrator's award (as well as the judgment of the Superior Court) as violating due process and in derogation of the primary jurisdiction of the National Labor Relations Board, which upholds and enforces the rights and duties of the parties under national labor law. On each of these points, our side had ample authority to support it. On the constitutional point, we had solid precedent, and on the jurisdictional question there was a growing body of developing law that bolstered our position. The case was a cinch.

Rarely does a lawyer come across the so-called "purple cow" -- a case that is "on all fours" with the case that he is arguing, both in fact and in law. Such a case, fortunately, had been decided by a California appellate court but a few years before. Coincidentally, it involved another Retail Clerks' local, and the facts were indistinguishable from those in the MORE Thriftimart matter. When I showed it to the lawyer for Thriftimart, he, too, felt that it would be downhill for us from then on.[10] When, I filed the petition on behalf of MORE in federal court, the clerk drew from his box the name of the venerable Judge Matthew Byrne, Sr. I had previously had a matter before Judge Byrne, when I had sought an injunction against another labor union. Based upon the law and the facts in that earlier case, I was clearly then entitled to such relief. But Judge Byrne had had other ideas. His action, or rather inaction, in that particular matter reflected that even when a court deliberately dons the robes of "inactive," it makes law. Although precedent allowed, even required, that the union be enjoined in that particular situation, Judge Byrne, after showing me in chambers his withdrawal card from the Brickmasons Union many years before, stated that he had a policy of not giving preliminary injunctions except in "falling wall" situations, and then only if the wall were likely to fall within the next hour.

---

[10]The only other "purple cow" I had encountered until that time was very early in my practice, when my prospective client was a sweet little old lady (yes, from Pasadena). She was the widowed owner of an eight-unit apartment house. A woman tenant acted as her agent in exchange for, initially one-quarter, then one-half, and finally a full, deduction of rent. After these arrangements had gone on for many years, this tenant, with the help of the California Labor Commissioner, sued my intended client for years of back pay at overtime rates since she allegedly had to stay continually in her apartment to await prospective tenants; like a fireman, she was allegedly always at work. After listening to the facts, I felt that the Labor Commissioner was acting capriciously against this sweet little old lady. I saw no way in which $11,000 in back wages "owed" by this lady by a decision of the Labor Commissioner could be sustained. That is, until I researched the cases and found one exactly on point involving another little old lady with another eight-unit apartment building who also had a lawyer who thought as I did. He lost the whole kit and caboodle before the California appellate court. The only difference in our cases was that the apartment houses were on different streets. Ruefully armed with this authority, I was not thereafter surprised to learn that I was the eighth attorney this little old lady had sought to engage. After advising her of the hopelessness of her cause, I rejected her case.

In view of that previous encounter with Judge Byrne, and knowing his narrow view of his own jurisdiction in a labor dispute context, his subsequent action in the MORE case did not take me totally by surprise. He listened patiently to my arguments and, in open court, stated, "Mr. Tobin,.you are absolutely right. The arbitrator did not have the right to render his award, nor did the Superior Court have the right to affirm that award. Nor do I have the right to tell you what I just told you, because I lack jurisdiction. I am therefore dismissing the case." In other words, I was clearly right, but had no remedy because nobody could tell me that officially. I was right without a right! Rarely had I been so complimented and with such courtesy kicked out the door at the same time. This strange "non-activist" doctrine, however, bypassed, if it did not overrule, some 150 years of jurisprudence in this country.

Still, the best I could do under the circumstances was to appeal. But to whom? Should I stay in the federal court or go back to the state court? In the early 1960s, it was generally considered by labor law practitioners that as bad as state courts were in understanding labor law, the federal courts were worse. So with somewhat less cockiness on my part, and notably less confidence in me on the part of my client, I decided to troop back to the state appellate court to appeal the decision of the superior court which had confirmed the award.

But I decided that, before doing so, I would probably have a good crack at achieving my ends by filing a charge with the National Labor Relations Board, asserting that the union by this arbitration award was attempting to force employees into a union against their free choice. No one in this entire matter ever denied that the employees were merely pawns and had no desire to be represented by the union. But that point, which some visitor from Mars might naively have presumed was the main point of the litigation, was beside the point.

Once again, I was stymied. The NLRB ruled that it could not issue a complaint against the union because the union had not yet attempted to enforce the award. Of course, the Clerks were threatening to bring a damage action seeking back pay from the company, but no matter, that wasn't enough for the NLRB. So, six months later, I did bring my appeal to the appellate court in California. Needless to say, my client, who had entered my representation with the highest hopes and guarantees, now looked at me somewhat askance. But onward I marched, knowing that victory was just ahead: There was indeed "a light at the end of the tunnel," a phrase that was soon to become popular elsewhere.

Briefs were filed by all parties, and within a year the matter (now two years since its inception) was scheduled for oral argument. It was now 1961, Governor Pat Brown was sitting in Sacramento, and judges were being appointed to higher positions every day. An opening occurred on the state Supreme Court, and lo and behold, there appeared a front-page article in the Los Angeles Herald Express, written by the Retail Clerks' president, urging that the Governor appoint a woman to that court and praising the virtues of Mildred Lillie, then on the Court of Appeals. He knew, as I did, that this same Judge Lillie would be one of the three judges hearing the case of Thriftimart v. Retail Clerks the following week.

My faith in ultimate justice was to receive still another fresh wound. The case was argued before a three-judge appellate court panel that included Lillie, and a decision was rendered quickly in favor of the union. The "indistinguishable case" that I referred to -- the purple cow -- turned out to have been an apparition. The court disposed of that authority by purportedly "distinguishing" it from the facts before it. To this day, I have found no one who has found any merit whatsoever in such a distinction. (Lillie, strangely, never got promoted.)[11]

---

[11] Some years later, President Nixon was desirous of appointing the first woman to the United States Supreme Court. Lillie was among those seriously considered.

Notwithstanding this unfathomable but clearly adverse decision, in Alfred E. Newman fashion I expressed unbounded determination (even optimism) to take the case to the state Supreme Court. My client's reaction to this was a heightened reluctance to continue to pay my fees. I spent many hours, with all the charm and conviction I could muster, prevailing upon my client to permit me to go on. Indeed, my client's potential liability increased daily and it seemed as if only my enthusiasm stood between it and bankruptcy.

I pushed on and filed a petition for review before the state Supreme Court. Though less than one in ten cases was and is granted review, the entire court agreed to hear the matter. Many months later, we gave oral argument before that court. I had good reason to be confident because when the entire court agrees to review a lower court's decision, it usually reverses that court, and the lower court was so patently in error it could hardly be defended.

The State Supreme Court then had an excellent reputation and was adorned by some of the best legal minds that ever favored any state court. It was then, and even more so in later years, described as an "activist" court. To some extent this was true, but, then that term was not necessarily pejorative. While he was not yet the Chief Justice, the court's most illustrious member was Justice Roger Traynor. He was so brilliant that often I and many other attorneys would happily sit in the courtroom and hear cases unrelated to our own practices, simply to witness a first-class mind in operation.

My argument before the Court started innocently; Traynor playfully toyed with my Boston accent. My opening sentence was, "The pattern in this case is clear, your Honor." When I said this in my Boston birthright brogue, it caused Traynor, who had wit as well as wisdom, to interrupt me and say, "Counsel, I thought this was a labor case. I did not know it was a patent case." The entire courtroom laughed, and it was some time before I was able to comprehend why.

Before long, the levity disappeared and the colloquy between me and the court became somewhat more ominous. My main weapon was the due process argument, that no decision affecting MORE or its employees could or should be enforced if they did not have the opportunity to participate or even be invited to the arbitration, especially since they were the ones most affected. Not only did I have sound California authority for this proposition, but the United States Constitution was unequivocal, it seemed to me. Yet Traynor and his brethren were disinclined to hear that particular argument -- my main point. They kept indicating that I should direct my attention to my second, somewhat weaker, point -- that the arbitrator and the state court did not have jurisdiction on this, a labor relations representational matter.

I wanted to go in the direction where I was strong, to hammer home the due process argument. The Court wanted to hear from me on my somewhat less than strong point (since, in the months before oral argument was had, some court decisions had been mildly disconcerting on this issue). Usually, in arguing before a court, a good lawyer will try to take a pliable stance: "Yes, sir, boss, anything you say." But I did not like where the Court was veering; I wanted to win. Unlike the wise bamboo, in this instance I did not bend with the wind. I failed to follow the Court's direction to bypass my principal point and discuss my secondary one. My presentation was definitely not an example of good appellate practice, particularly for one who had formerly taught an appellate argument course to law school students.

Traynor especially seemed determined to have the court rule on the representational question. He yearned to enunciate what the law should be in that area. His views differed from mine. In addition to being one of the great state court justices of this century, he had special talent in matters involving labor relations and had been a pathfinder in shaping labor law, not only in California but throughout the country.

When the oral argument was over, I was upset with myself for resisting in unseemly fashion the Court's direction. Though I did not realize it then, Traynor and the Court had already decided to uphold my due process argument. In fact, they dismissed the rationale of the court below almost perfunctorily.

The Court decided unanimously in my favor. In its published opinion, however, the Court also did what it -- or at least Justice Traynor -- had intended all along. This case exemplifies what courts are prone to do despite the tenets of sound jurisprudence. In the lengthy opinion, the Court devoted the first 90 percent of its discussion to my second argument, the jurisdictional issue, in which it found against me. Only in the final two paragraphs, almost summarily, did it uphold my principal argument, due process.

Properly, the Court should have written a one-paragraph decision on the due process issue and stopped. Justice Traynor, however, believed that the jurisdictional issue should be clarified in accordance with what he considered to be sound labor relations law. He therefore went out of his way to devise, analyze, and enunciate a preemption or jurisdictional rule. Interestingly, his view on this issue was seemingly accepted by most courts for many years, but today the "prevailing" rule is as clouded as it ever was. The case, therefore, remains an example of what a court will often do when it has another axe to grind and is not simply seeking to reach a just result in the matter before it. In this case, fortuitously, "justice" was achieved, but by a very roundabout route.

* * * * *

Courts will not only bend jurisprudential safeguards to attain intended ends, they are not above playing loose with the facts to aid their aims. In using the otherwise effective "case method," law schools do <u>not</u> teach that judges, like most of the rest of us, will reach conclusions or write opinions that usually appear to be perfectly logical and reasonable based upon selected facts discussed in those opinions. The premised "facts," however, may often be incidental or even contrary to the actual record. By this, I do not mean those facts that are in dispute. Disputed facts obviously have to be decided for or against the parties, right or wrong. But courts are not immune to ignoring or torturing facts that do not fit in with their programmed course of action. Procrustean justice may be an oxymoron, but it is not an infrequent practice.

Even the United States Supreme Court has been guilty of such a practice. My first major case before that court occurred in 1964, when I had been an attorney for less than five years. National Labor Relations Board v. Servette was the first case involving the interpretation of the Landrum-Griffin Act to reach that Court. Congress, in 1959, had passed this important labor legislation, originally introduced by Senator John F. Kennedy but then disavowed by him because the legislative process had turned it, arguably, to the labor unions' disadvantage.

Servette, a distributor/vendor of products to supermarket chains, had lost its case before the NLRB on a stipulated record. At that point, I began representing the company and was successful in convincing the Circuit Court of Appeals to reverse the Board's decision. Because the case was of national importance, the Supreme Court granted a review of the matter. One of the critical underlying factors, involving the legality of secondary boycotts, was whether individual store managers, apart from their chains, could decide to purchase products from vendors such as Servette.

Servette, a non-union company, ran up against the Teamsters Union, which naturally opposed any such company supplying supermarkets. To gain its ends, the Teamsters engaged in a secondary boycott against those supermarkets that Servette serviced. It did so both by handbilling the public not to patronize the markets and by coercing some store managers not to accept or buy Servette products. There was no evidence whatsoever in the record that these managers had the authority to decide whether to do business with Servette. There was, however, uncontradicted evidence that it was only their superiors who could make these decisions. Accordingly, the language of the statute seemingly dictated that such coercive action by the union was unlawful. And I so argued. I lost.[12]

The Supreme Court properly sought to provide an interpretation and clarification of this new legislation because of its national significance. The Court knew the end it sought to reach. It held that such secondary boycotts (particularly handbilling in the context of free speech) were permissible, and that attempts to coerce managerial employees were also legal since these managers could make the decision as to whether to deal with the vendor with whom the union had a dispute. The fact that in this case the evidence did not support that assumption and that these managers did not have this decision-making power, did not bother the Court. It simply accepted the NLRB's assertion, contrary to the uncontroverted evidence that indicated

---

[12] An interesting sidelight to this case was that my opposing counsel was the Solicitor General, Archibald Cox, appearing in his cutaways. Interestingly enough, although I had audited one of his courses at Harvard Law School a few years before, he treated me with the same polite but indigenous condescension as he would have any of his students: he made his oral argument to the Court from handwritten notes on the back of an envelope! In addition to being the nation's foremost labor law teacher, he had an additional advantage over me. He and Justice Goldberg, who was then sitting on the bench, had been the principal labor advisors to Senator Kennedy and had drafted the ambiguous legislation!

A second reminiscence of this case (for trivia buffs) was that Justice Black, well along in age, appeared to be dozing while Cox and I were arguing. But when I raised a seldom cited case, Giboney v. Empire Storage & Ice Co., which restricted free speech and which Black had written 15 years before and had regretted ever since, he awoke. His back stiffened, he looked at me searchingly and began asking difficult questions. Apocryphally, at least, he would now awaken from his grave if a possible First Amendment limitation were raised even (or especially) in prayer.

they had no such authority. There is no judicial appeal from the Supreme Court.

* * * * *

What do these cases tell us about the process of, and quest for, justice? Primarily, that the course is likely to be long, circuitous, and on occasion, a wild goose chase. The reward of the hunt will, in the end, be judged from multiple perspectives:

Justice -- to the union in the MORE/Thriftimart case was having its expansive interpretation of a contract upheld. The union posed as the great defender of the sanctity of contracts -- ironically, the escutcheon of the nineteenth-century capitalists.

Justice -- to the employer was having its employees' rights upheld -- on its face at least, is as often suspicious as it is sincere.

Justice -- to the arbitrator ended up being a surprise -- to both parties.

Justice -- to the Superior Court was whatever justice was to the arbitrator.

Justice -- to the federal district court was something that it piously recognized, but unofficially opined was beyond its bailiwick.

Justice -- to the NLRB, a sophisticated bureaucracy, was something, but not yet ripe.

Justice -- to the state appellate court was simple but inexplicable.

Justice -- to the state Supreme Court in MORE/Thriftimart - was upholding the Constitution -- and establishing bold, venturesome labor law doctrine that would shape events beyond the state's borders.

And justice -- to the United States Supreme Court, as served up in Servette, was to create national law -- the facts, when necessary to that purpose, being rendered irrelevant.

In 1864, exactly one hundred years prior to the time that the California Supreme Court and the United States Supreme Court each separately decided MORE/Thriftimart and Servette, Abraham Lincoln nominated Salmon P. Chase as Chief Justice to the nation's highest court. Daniel Donald, in his recent heralded study of our greatest President, has written that Lincoln at the time stated his hope that "the new Chief Justice would recognize that 'the function of the courts is to decide cases -- not principles.'" Fat chance.

The epilogue to these cases:

Within a year after the California Supreme Court decided in favor of MORE, the MORE stores bellied up for reasons having little to do with the case. What is far more important, after three decades and thousands of germane cases in California and elsewhere, Traynor's position as to a state's jurisdiction in this type of labor case is just as often ignored as followed.

And over thirty years after the Supreme Court "clarified" the legislative intent surrounding the 1959 Congressional legislation involved in Servette, courts throughout the country, including the Supreme Court itself, were still wrestling with the confusion created by that clarification.[13]

Rashomon, meet Sisyphus.

---

[13] The Supreme Court years later decided Edward J. De Bartolo Co. v. Florida Gulf Coast Building & Construction Trades Commission, a case that had been winding through the Board and the courts for almost a decade. The main issues in that case revolved around those seemingly decided and laid to rest the day Servette was decided. But in 1988, in De Bartolo, the Court's ruling made its pronouncements and rationale in 1964 (exactly twenty-four years to the day) virtually irrelevant and meaningless.

Chapter 17.

The JFK Assassination Miasma:
A Conspiracy of Lawyers

A Lawyer's Holiday

It was an alluring possibility. Some three weeks after the traumatic events in Dallas, I received a serious inquiry as to whether I would be interested in joining the investigative staff of the Warren Commission. My then current responsibilities did not permit it, and, with regret, I declined. This, then, was one "legal" experience that pretty much got away.

But I did continue to muse about it. After all, for a young lawyer, this would have been a golden opportunity. More importantly, the assassination of President Kennedy was surely one of the most significant events in the nation's history, at least in this century. To ascertain the cause of such a tragedy was important to the American people; the safety of the country and the credibility of its leaders and institutions were at stake. The Kennedy persona, legacy and myth, which were gradually galvanizing the nation, would, it appeared clear, magnify and magnetize in the generations to come.

Still another factor caused me sadness in turning away from the chance of helping to uncover history. Aside from being a lifelong history buff and sharing JFK's geographic and educational background and political outlook, my affinity for and contact with him had been longstanding. While still a teenager in high school in 1946, I delivered campaign brochures to voters in his first election to the House of Representatives. Six years later, as president of the Harvard Democratic Club, I was successful in having the Liberal Union reverse its position supporting Henry Cabot Lodge in Kennedy's hard fought but successful race to unseat Senator Lodge. (Liberals then couldn't stomach Joe Kennedy and they seemed to think that the umbilical cord between father and son couldn't be cut.)

Throughout the years that followed, very many thoughtful observers came to realize that John Kennedy was increasingly becoming a lodestar for the political (and often personal) hopes and yearnings of millions of people. My personal contacts with him in the years after college were, however, both infrequent and, with a couple of exceptions, mostly casual. One encounter, however, is still vividly etched in my memory and on the night of November 22, 1963 came once again clearly into focus. At the Harvard Commencement on June 14, 1956, Kennedy was being awarded an honorary degree by his alma mater. Even for a Kennedy, this was considered ennobling; he was obviously proud. But I learned that day what he meant, in part at least, when he used the expression "grace under pressure."

Whether out of respect for his office, his mien or just legendary Harvard indifference, of the hundreds of alumni present in The Yard before the procession began to the Tercentenary Theatre for the formal commencement events, no one approached within twenty yards of Senator Kennedy. I peered in his direction, noticing that he was having some difficulty putting on his academic gown and doctoral insignia. Thinking I could be of some aid, I went up to him and offered a helping hand. He appeared in a state of discomfort; his face grimaced; his brow was moist. I started to assist him when he politely said - with a strained smile - that he could handle the chore. I drew back. He continued to twist and turn in an attempt to compel his body and the garment to act in concert. Then, even from a distance of many feet, I could see him begin to perspire profusely. The endeavor was for him plainly painful. His pride, however, was, just as plainly, dominant. I kept my distance. Finally, after still minutes more of travail, his task was accomplished.

Though his plight in these situations was one, I am sure, he continually fought to keep private, when he realized that I had witnessed his successful struggle, he smiled broadly, as would a little boy, who had just, for the first time, found that, despite the precariousness surrounding the effort, he really could negotiate that two-wheeler. For years, Kennedy bore the onus of a back that continually brought pain and almost caused his death. That suffering would end only when someone situated in the southeastern corner of the sixth floor of a non-descript building on Elm Street in Dallas, for reasons that will always remain speculative, repeatedly squeezed the trigger of a 1940 Monnelicher-Carcano rifle.

While I had resigned myself to not participating in an official account of the Kennedy assassination, I took an avid interest in the Commission's investigation. For some 30 years, from the sidelines and, on occasion, as an actual participant in "re-creation," I proceeded to marshal the available facts, weigh the multitudinous arguments, the plausible and implausible, and to ponder some of the imponderables. This personal, if vicarious, expedition is a lawyer's holiday. It could not be taken lightly, however; for the entire probe had come to take on a dramatic dimension - soon to become a spectacle: the most agonizing pursued "who-done-it" in world history. In time, this probe, with the political and theatrical baggage attending it, has become a point thrust in challenge to the very core of our democratic tenets.

Unless and until this continuing inquest leads to a consensus and a rational assessment of the critical issues raised by the assassination, the stability of the realm - haunted by a Banquo's Ghost - will suffer. Lawyers in this <u>non-legal</u> dispute, because of their special involvement in the inquest and their concern for an ordered society, have a need to help bring about such a resolution.

The Investigators: Lawyers on Trial

Lawyers, from the outset and throughout the over three decades of Kennedy assassination mania, have taken center stage in the massive and multiple investigations that have enveloped the nation since Dallas. And, in keeping with their reputation, lawyers have spent tens of millions of taxpayers' dollars and endless time in this search for answers. Following right on their backs, making mega-bucks and international reputations, have come the novelists and dramatists in their effort to undermine those proffered answers. A cottage industry has developed into an international phenomenon.

Lawyers, however, whatever their other characteristics, are especially qualified to conduct such investigations. By training and experience, they are skilled in probing, ferreting out, weighing and distilling facts and then organizing, presenting and making conclusions from them. While subjectivity naturally enters the process, lawyers are guided to and judged by the objectivity of the end product. Any lawyer will vouch that the first and foremost assurance of success - even more than legal knowledge - is having the facts on his side; getting them right is almost always more important than iron-clad guarantees of the payment of his fees.

It is not surprising, therefore, that one week after assuming the presidency, Lyndon Johnson appointed seven men, all lawyers, headed by the Chief Justice, to what was thereafter known as the Warren Commission. In the decade before that Commission issued its report in September 1964, the battlecry of those on the far right had been, "Impeach Earl Warren." In the decades afterwards, from various points on the spectrum, it sounded like "Impeach the Warren Commission." Though some of those appointees had been outstanding lawyers, prosecutors, or judges, their strength was based upon their generally uncanny ability to understand and appreciate the complexities of society and the intricacies of constitutional government. More importantly, it is almost impossible to imagine any group of men that would have commanded greater respect for fairness and integrity.

Though these Commission members devoted unusual amounts of time to the task before them - they hardly could be accused of laxity - the bulk of the grinding, painstaking and professional labor rested upon the legal staff. All 15 counsel to the Commission were not only savvy and experienced lawyers, but combined, this crême-de-la-crême group would have formed one of the most formidable law firms in the nation. This brilliant array of talent was supported by another tier of staff members, covering a number of specialties, including lawyers; again, the credentials of these individuals were outstanding. Still other highly able persons, many attorneys included, lent further support to carry out LBJ's instruction to the Commission "to satisfy itself that the truth [become] known as far as it can be discovered." Overseeing (if not policing), and certainly cooperating with the Commission, was the Attorney General's office, led by Robert Kennedy and supported by numerous JFK stalwarts, including Nicholas Katzenbach and other highly reputable attorneys. In fact, Robert Kennedy had Attorney Howard Willens appointed to the Commission both to serve that body and to act as the liaison to the Justice Department.

Ten months later, the Commission issued its Report. It did so in some 27 volumes of analyses, collected data, evidence, exhibits and testimony (of 552 witnesses). No one has ever seriously charged any Commissioner with lacking innate intelligence. The attack upon the Commission has hardly been so polite.

Conspiracy In A Nutshell

Virtually none of the essential facts uncovered in the Commission's (and subsequent) investigations has gone unchallenged by its critics-at-large. All of its major findings and conclusions are not only roundly attacked but endlessly ridiculed. Just about the only common ground surrounding Dealey Plaza is that Abraham Zapruder's film captures a significant and accurate part of the story. Even that agreement is but a starting point, as the film, itself is subject to profoundly different interpretations -- Rashomon-in-reverse.

The crux of the Commission's conclusions is that, in a nutshell:
1) Lee Harvey Oswald;
2) acting alone;
3) shot and killed President Kennedy and wounded Governor John Connally;
4) from the sixth floor of the Texas School Book Depository;
5) by firing three shots from a Monnelicher-Carcano Italian rifle, which he owned.

It follows, à fortiori (as lawyers and Latins would put it), that if these conclusions are true, all else that the Commission found or didn't find - including the killings of both Dallas policeman J.D. Tippet and Oswald, himself, by Jack Ruby and the whole kit-and-caboodle of allegations, speculations and hobgoblins that followed in the wake of the assassination - are mere capillaries, footnotes to history.

The case in support of the Commission's theses was extremely well documented and logical. Of course, the size of a brief or even its logic are not hallmarks of truth. Despite their imposing portfolios, it is conceivable that these men were collectively hoodwinked and the Commission simply served as a "patsy" for smarter and more powerful forces. An examination of all available facts made known to the Commission, or credible evidence brought forth by others, however, lends little credence to the underlying accusation that the Commission was incompetent. An analysis of the components of each of the Commission's conclusions just noted puts the critics, not the Commissioners or lawyers on trial.

The first key proposition advanced by the Commission is that Oswald shot and killed Kennedy. If he did so, it follows that he did so by firing his 6.5 millimeter rifle from the sixth floor of the Book Depository building. If this basic proposition is accepted, half of the problem posed to the world is resolved. Of the many critics (coming from all directions), only the most rabid and least credible have stated or titillatingly implied that Oswald did not shoot Kennedy. Only those whose feet are stuck in stone could fail to recognize that the Commission's case on this point is overwhelming. In fact, the burden of proof it had to carry was not that imposed in a criminal case. Essentially, it was called upon to render a verdict by a preponderance of the evidence. Nonetheless, so powerful was its evidence on this first key proposition, that it not only passed a "beyond-a-reasonable-doubt" test but proved this point "beyond-a-shadow-of-a-doubt."

The massive evidence to support this finding included: (1) an eyewitness who, immediately following the shooting, testified to a man fitting Oswald's description with a rifle at the window on the sixth floor of the TSBD building at precisely the time of the assassination; (2) others who saw a rifle being fired from that location at the exact time; (3) Oswald was described by other witnesses as being present on the sixth floor of that building just before the assassination; (4) the fact that he was still in the building minutes afterwards, at a distance from the sixth floor window where shots were fired and from which he could have easily travelled in the intervening time; (5) the bullets that killed Kennedy (and wounded Connally) -- according to undisputed expert evidence -- came from the Monnelicher-Carcano rifle to the exclusion of all other weapons; (6) the wounds received by Kennedy which caused his death were fired from above and behind the Presidential limousine; (7) Oswald had bought, owned, and had in his possession on that day that rifle; (8) Oswald brought that weapon to work that morning wrapped in an improvised paper bag (which he referred to as "curtain rods"); (9) undisputed expert testimony proved that Oswald's palm print and no one else's prints were found on that rifle; (10) both the weapon and the paper bag were later found, following the assassination, partially hidden in separate areas, but near the window where shots were fired from the sixth floor; (11) undisputed expert testimony showed that three used cartridge cases, fired from the same rifle owned and possessed by Oswald and from the same rifle that fired the bullets that hit Kennedy and Connally -- to the exclusion of all other weapons --were found on the floor next to the window on the sixth floor from where the shots were fired; (12) witnesses on the 5th floor of the same building heard shots from the sixth floor window area and cartridges falling to the floor from that spot at the time of the shooting; (13) Based upon the testimony and testing by experts and other supporting evidence, a person of Oswald's capabilities could have fired the shots from that rifle in the time frame of the assassination; (14) earlier that year, according to credible evidence given to the Commission by Oswald's wife, he attempted to kill retired General Edwin Walker in Texas, thus demonstrating his willingness to take human life (perhaps for political reasons); (15) Officer J.D. Tippet was killed 45 minutes after JFK. Nine eyewitnesses positively identified Oswald as the man they saw shoot Officer Tippet or leave the scene with the revolver that killed him -- one owned by Oswald and in his possession when captured. Additional evidence conclusively proved that Oswald killed Tippet. (16) Though the Commission did not specifically so find, all the evidence before it failed to show (a) that other than Oswald, anyone else, with or without a weapon, was seen on the sixth floor by anyone prior to the shooting; (b) or during the shooting; (c) or that anyone else left the sixth floor or the building immediately after the shooting of Kennedy; (17) a host of additional incriminating facts, (e.g., his prints on the cartons next to the window, his clipboard later found hidden behind another nearby carton) added to this mountain of evidence.

The more rational critics generally concede that the Commission was undoubtedly right on this score and are quick to criticize and dissociate themselves from those who would avoid incontestable facts and engage in flights of fancy. These somewhat more responsible critics, however, take issue with the second key conclusion of the Commission: Oswald was the sole assassin, and the corollary findings that three shots -- and only three shots -- were fired, all from the window of the sixth floor on the southeastern corner of the TSBD building and that these shots caused the death of Kennedy and the wounding of Connally. Who wins this one essentially carries the day.

The evidence supporting the Commission on this paramount point is powerful and persuasive -- but not conclusive. Its essential ingredients are: (1) all the shots were from the rear; (2) in all probability, there were no more nor fewer than three shots; (3) they all emanated from the sixth floor of the TSBD; (4) one bullet, likely the first shot, struck Kennedy in the back of the neck; one shot missed entirely, causing no harm or damage to anyone or anything; another bullet entered the right-rear portion of his head, "causing a massive and fatal wound" and; (5) no other shots were fired from any other location.

Most critics scoff at one, more, or all of these conclusions. They have advanced three main contentions. First, the Zapruder film depicts that the shot that struck Kennedy in the skull caused his head to move sharply backward. This, according to one set of critics (with another set of critics in complete disagreement), clearly proves that Kennedy was shot from the front, i.e., there was a second assassin. Aside from the fact that the medical evidence and pathological testimony were both voluminous and unanimous that the bullet to Kennedy's head came from the rear, the jerking backward movement lends little or no credence to the critics' case. Subsequent ballistic and medical testimony, and separate experimentations with animals showed that such head movement could easily be caused by nerve damage, bringing about muscle tightening, resulting in a rearward movement. Indeed, some twenty years after the Commission's report, studies undertaken by independent experts showed that "an object struck in the rear by a high-velocity missle similar to the bullets that hit Kennedy always falls backward as a result of the jet-propulsion effect created by tissues exploding out the front."

The rest of these frontal attacks relate to the centerpiece of the Commission's Report -- the "single-bullet theory." The Zapruder film makes it reasonably clear that the time span between the first and last shot to have hit Kennedy was between 4.18/5.6 and seven-plus seconds. If the second of three shots missed, then the total span between the first and last shot would be no more than 5.6 seconds. It would, therefore, have been possible, but unlikely, for Oswald to have first shot Kennedy in the back of the neck, then hit Connally, and then shot Kennedy in the back of the head, in that expert evidence showed the Commission that it would take a minimum of 2.3 seconds for a person to operate the rifle from one shot to the next. Equally significant -- and a separate way to reach the same conclusion -- is that the Zapruder film also showed it took less than two seconds between observable reactions by Kennedy from his neck wound and from Connally following his wounds. Thus, unless there was a second assassin, the single bullet proposition found by the Commission becomes crucial to its conclusions.

Paradoxically, even if the Commission's "single-bullet" theory is undermined, the "second assassin" advocates still have their own problem. Aside from that fact, as the Commission found, that there is no credible evidence of anyone seeing another gunman in and around Dealey Plaza, (a) what happened to the bullet that entered and exited Kennedy's neck from the rear? It did not hit anyone or anything (other than Connally); and (b) the bullet that hit Connally came from the rear and was yawing (meaning it went through something or someone else first); (c) the bullet that hit Connally came from the same rifle found on the sixth floor of the TSBD; (d) three spent cartridges, from that same rifle, were found at the southeastern corner window of that same building; no cartridges of any kind were found elsewhere. (e) the wounds Connally suffered could hardly, scientifically, have been caused in any other manner. But the single-bullet thesis stands up on its own affirmative merits. The Warren Commission had before it expert medical and ballistic evidence that the trajectory of a bullet's path between the sixth floor of the TSBD building and the wounds suffered by JFK and Connally were in alignment; that the path of the wounds between JFK and Connally was consistent with a single bullet; that the bullet found on Connally's stretcher at the hospital in the condition it was when recovered was not inconsistent with that bullet causing all of Connally's wounds after first passing through Kennedy in the manner it did. In fact, this same evidence made it difficult to explain how Connally could have suffered the wounds he did other than as concluded by the Commission.

Undaunted, most of the critics continued to attempt to undermine the single (they call it the "magic") bullet thesis. They first rely upon Connally's own testimony that he heard the first shot, turned towards the rear, not having been hit by that shot but rather by a later bullet. The Governor was consistent and unequivocal on this point -- he repeatedly stated it. Medical testimony -- as well as considerable anecdotal evidence -- responded that quite often victims of wounds are unaware of them for brief and sometimes considerable periods thereafter. The Commission so found in this situation.

Some critics also argued that the Zapruder film negates even the possibility that Kennedy and Connally were physically aligned so as to allow a single bullet to cause the effect claimed. "There was just no way in the world that the bullet could have done that," repeated one leading critic, whose pronouncement was echoed and broadcast as though it were the Holy Gospel. In fact, the Commission conducted elaborate experiments to ascertain the alignment between JFK and Connally in relationship to the trajectory of the shots from the sixth floor window of the Depository. Additional tests by other experts in ballistics buttressed the findings of the alignment testimony, indicating, if not conclusively, that the single-bullet theory was very likely correct.

Finally, the critics ridicule the proposition that the same bullet could have entered JFK from the back of his neck, exited beneath his Adam's apple, then entered Connally's back, traversed through his chest, exited below the right nipple, pierced the back of his arm near the wrist, struck the surface of the wrist bone, exited the surface of the palm and then punctured his thigh, causing a slight tangential wound. This was essentially the bullet found on Connally's stretcher at the Parkland Hospital. Thus, the "magic" bullet. As Congressman Richardson Preyer would later state in this very same context many years later:

> "Listening to all of the evidence that we have heard here today on the behavior of bullets, I must say it impresses on me once again the limits of common sense. Common sense tells us that no bullet could do anything like that; but common sense tells us the world is flat, too, and we know the world is round, and so I think there are limits to how rationally we can think about the course of this bullet under such circumstances."

The ballistics experts before the Commission conducted numerous examinations and measurements. They then performed simulated re-enactments of the assassination and comparable tests of wounds to similar flesh and bones and came to the conclusion that a single bullet probably accounted for all these wounds. The weight of the recovered bullet on the stretcher was slightly less than it was when it was fired. The small fragments found in Connally's wrist wound were significantly less in weight than the difference. Reviewing all this testing data and adding medical input, two highly qualified doctors concluded that it was probable that the same bullet had passed through JFK's neck and then caused all the wounds to Connally. They also asserted that, had the bullet not first hit Kennedy, Connally's wrist injury would have been far more extensive.

The Commission had spoken. Its critics, as perceptive observers predicted from the beginning, quickly began to shoot at it from every conceivable angle. Lee Harvey Oswald was never tried, but the Warren Commission has been on trial from the day it began its thankless task. The Commission, its staff, and the innumerable private citizen-experts who supported its conclusions, have been called everything from willing dupes to deliberate liars, but at the very least dishonest and/or incompetent. The American public, most of which was later weaned on Watergate and Viet Nam and then Iran-Contra, started to suspect another cover-up and, at the very least, a conspiracy -- of some sort. Healthy skepticism began yielding to bellicose cynicism.

On An Attorney's Agenda: Voir-dire

Soon after the Commission's Report was issued, I became disturbed by the incipient but insipid criticism it had begun to receive in some quarters. After all, these attacks upon the integrity and competence of the Commission were, in large part, salvos against lawyers (and the best of them) and lawyer-like work, as well as going to the very core of our constitutional government. Lawyers, who are vested with the duty to uphold society's laws, were, by insinuation, being accused of what is tantamount to regicide. At the same time, I was troubled by a few important points which I felt were unresolved or unclear, even after reading the Commission's lengthy report. To meet these two separate concerns, within the next few months I undertook to study most of the supporting volumes to the Report and to read and understand the written criticism of it coming off the presses.

After a few months doing this "homework" only a couple of issues going to the validity of the Report remained in doubt. Fortuitously, I was invited to address a client-association that was having its convention in Dallas in March, 1965, less than six months after the Report was issued. It was a splendid opportunity to engage in a "hands-on" inspection of Dealey Plaza. It was what lawyers might call voir-dire, to see-hear for myself; to give my analysis an element of authority. I packed the Report and a couple of critical articles into my briefcase and left an extra day or two on my itinerary to do "my thing."

When I went to the Book Depository, from the outside, it looked as pictured and the work inside appeared to be as it had been described before that fateful day. As I slowly edged into the first floor, briefcase in hand, I did not expect to be able to venture much further into this historical but then private edifice. To my surprise, the dozen or so people working there paid absolutely no attention to me. Boldly, I walked the full length of that floor, boarded the elevator, punched the button and was on my way to the sixth floor. No one was on the sixth floor; a dozen or so cartons and boxes were strewn around; very little, if anything, appeared to have been changed since November 22, 1963.

For the next couple of hours, I checked out what were thought to have been Oswald's movements in that building on that fateful day. First I went to the window, and spent considerable time reviewing the charts and photos published by the Commission, did various measurements, and eyed open cars heading toward the overpass on Elm Street. My military tour in Korea was as an historian, not a sharpshooter. Still, firing an M-1 was the one soldierly assignment I ever did with proficiency. Simulating rifle fire, from that window, I was confident that with or without a telescopic lens, it was not too difficult a task to fire accurately two out of three shots at a man in an open car some 70 yards directly ahead. (A CBS conducted test about a year later suggested it was generally more difficult than I or the Commission judged it to be -- but still quite possible and not unlikely for a good marksman.) I then checked out the areas where Oswald had left the Monnelicher-Carcano and scope and where he hid the improvised paper bag and his clipboard.

Then I timed myself, at a fast walk, descending the stairs to the second floor lunchroom. It took less than 90 seconds; again, in conformity with the time schedule set forth by the Commission. I then completed the exit route Oswald apparently took within the time span presented by the Commission before the front door was blocked by the Dallas police on that November day. My tour of the Depository building that day raised no new knowledge; it did afford me, however, the opportunity to "feel" the events the Commission depicted and to confirm their likelihood.

Standing now on Elm Street in front of the TSBD, I saw my main reason for inspecting the site of the assassination. Following the Commission's Report, it had become the focal point of the critics' scenario: the grassy knoll. The Commission hadn't treated that specific area with any special concern; it gave more attention to the Railroad Overpass, a site further removed. Though the evidence hardly left room for another assassin shooting from the front of the limousine, and though no witness actually testified as to seeing a gunman firing at the President from anywhere near the grassy knoll, many critics zeroed in on that plot of land, topped by a picket fence. The second assassin supposedly shot from behind that fence. Of course, given all the other evidence, such a shot, if it occurred, must have missed its mark completely. But many critics persisted -- perhaps faute de mieux -- based upon a supposed "puff of smoke" and the sighting of someone who later disappeared.

I inspected the grassy knoll and the now famous picket fence. One conclusion soon became obvious: it would have been almost impossible for a second assassin to have shot at Kennedy from anywhere in that vicinity. The Commission, apparently under the belief that it had so clearly proven the case of a single assassin from the rear, did not feel the need to prove a negative. It fairly limited its attention to the grassy knoll allegation to citing and discussing the evidence of the many witnesses in the area who saw no gunman or suspicious persons and the little evidence existing of possible gunfire emanating from that ground.

The topography of the knoll, its relation to the curvature of Elm Street and the angle of the fence itself, make it virtually impossible for any gunman (one who would have to have been over six feet tall, for that matter) to aim, let alone hit the President or Connally in the one or two seconds available for him to do so.

Further, such a "co-assassin" would have been forced to have stood upright, in clear view of a number of spectators and railway guards to his rear along the Railroad Overpass. According to the Zapruder film, he would, at best, have had his slim opportunity to have come even close to his target only after Kennedy had suffered both the neck wound and the shattering skull shot. In addition, any co-assassin's aim would have been further impaired at this point not only by Jacqueline Kennedy's body but by a half-dozen bystanders fleeing across the knoll. Thus, he would have instantly known that any shot he could have fired would have been as futile (and indeed, superfluous) as it would be suicidal.

While the Commission had presented considerable evidence proving that the trajectory of the rifle from the sixth floor window of the TSBD was consistent with the wounds of Kennedy and Connally, it was, I concluded, remiss in not conducting similar experiments from the grassy knoll. The results of such studies would readily demolish or at the very least derogate the keystone of its critics' case. The implausibility of the grassy knoll scenario would be manifest. I was surprised that it failed to do so and in the years since astonished that such a study has not been commissioned. If it were, it would have been far less likely that the conspiracy mania that has ensued would have gotten so out-of-hand and off-the-wall.

The Strange Meanderings of the Re-Examiners.

Though the Commission's critics never waned in their attacks, little material new evidence surfaced in the following decade. Their criticism, however, had the opposite effect of what they had sought. It played a part in Attorney General Ramsey Clark's inquest as to the role of the CIA in the "assassination plot;" but in 1968 he found that the CIA was not involved in any such "plot." As part of his investigation, he appointed a blue ribbon panel of pathologists, none having had any connection with the Warren Commission probe, to study all the facts. It did, and reaffirmed all the major findings of the 1964 investigation. Clark would be the last man on earth to exonerate the "right wing", the "establishment" or the CIA if he had any evidence of any kind of a "conspiracy". Later, in 1975, the Rockefeller Commission, studying the CIA, reached the same conclusion. Also in 1968, Jim Garrison, after a "zany" investigation and a ludicrous trial totally failed to convince a jury that any conspiracy existed or that a heretofore unknown man named Shaw was a part of it. Indeed, according to what he told Arthur Schlesinger Jr., it is fairly clear that Robert Kennedy, after conferring with one of his trusted lieutenants who was covering Garrison's opera bouffe in New Orleans, concluded that Garrison was a "fraud."

In the wake of Viet Nam and Watergate, Congress in 1976 began to stir. After two to three years of what appears to have been unusual political maneuvering, it established what, in effect, was a review board of the Warren Commission's findings. While that body, the House Select Committee on Assassins (Kennedy and Martin Luther King), and its staff were not entirely composed of lawyers, it was, as might be expected, again dominated by those with legal training and experience. This was the Committee that was expected to put to rest the conspiracy argument, one way or the other. If that was its mission, it should have gone back to balancing the budget.

The Committee, from its inception in 1976 and for at least two years thereafter had a rocky journey, not so much because of the controversial nature of its assignment but as a result of internal problems. Its mandate was limited in time and funding, each crimping a detached and in-depth probe. Moreover, the heavy turnover in its chairmanship, membership, counsel and staff, significantly impaired its efficiency and aggravated its timing and funding problems. Nonetheless, the twelve members of Congress persevered. They started by creating a number of panels of scientific experts who, in a professional and thorough manner, reviewed critical issues covered by the Warren Commission. These panels, in turn, presented their conclusions. The Committee then reviewed this often arcane and at times puzzling evidence and opinion and, in all but one singular instance, made well-balanced judgments.

The great irony in this long investigative odyssey is that the House Committee, while in vital areas conducting a more thorough investigation then did the Warren Commission, ended up by both clearly upholding and, simultaneously, plainly undermining the Warren Commission's critical conclusions. In the final analysis, the House Committee's Report can best be described as scholarly schizophrenia. This duplexity not only left the entire subject in a perpetual state of irresolution, but it enabled certain of the Warren Commission's rabid critics cleverly but improperly to portray the Committee's findings as supporting their own "far out" contentions.

The House Committee unequivocally found that Oswald killed Kennedy by firing three shots from the sixth floor of the TSBD. It further found that no other shot from any other direction hit the President or anyone else. Finally, relying upon still additional evidence that was unavailable to the Warren Commission, it concluded that Connally's wounds came from the same bullet that first struck Kennedy from the rear. In other words, it, too, solidly accepted and advanced the "single-bullet" theory -- undoubtedly the most crucial and controversial finding of the Warren Commission.

One would have thought that with these findings, the Committee's quest would have been fulfilled -- Q.E.D. It seemed that the two gunmen arguments had finally been put to rest -- at least officially. In fact, as late as December 1991, the Committee's Assistant Deputy Chief Counsel, Kenneth Klein, a highly regarded attorney, seemingly had no doubt that the Committee had indeed found that the evidence upheld the "lone assassin" conclusion of the Warren Commission. Listing the Committee's strong reasons for debunking the Commission's critics, Klein, in the Los Angeles Times, wrote:

> "Since the validity of the Warren Commission's finding that Lee Harvey Oswald was the lone assassin rested firmly on the validity of the single-bullet theory, the staff members of the select committee would have been thrilled to have disproved it. To have done so would surely have led to fame and fortune. Only one thing prevented us from doing so - the evidence."

But in the end, the House Committee did conclude there was "a high probability that two gunmen fired at" Kennedy. The Committee, by a divided and obviously wrenching vote, so ruled on December 29, 1978. Less than two weeks before, on December 18, the Committee had met and was on the verge of approving, perhaps unanimously, the first draft of its final report, which stated, "The committee finds that the available scientific evidence is insufficient that there was a conspiracy to assassinate President Kennedy." What caused this remarkable metamorphosis?

Acoustics. The Warren Commission did not avidly pursue the possible importance of a recording at the Dallas Police Department of sounds perhaps emanating from a motorcycle police microphone which might have been in Dealey Plaza at the time of the assassination. In 1963, there was scant scientific knowledge regarding this particular technology. Fifteen years later, some thought, the knowledge gained about the subject would enable the Committee to utilize the recording to ascertain the number of shots and their whereabouts that occurred in the Plaza that distant afternoon. The technical assignment was given by the Committee to a Boston consulting firm, supposedly one of the few sources with expertise-type credentials in this esoteric field. The consultant was directed to pinpoint and ascertain from the recording the likelihood of shots coming from both the Book Depository and the grassy knoll - the latter site being the critics' favorite spot from which, assertedly, a second assassin successfully fired a rifle shot at the President.

Early in 1978, the Committee's acoustic consultant, after conducting extensive experiments, concluded that indeed a motorcycle microphone, inadvertently stuck on "open," had recorded four rifle shots, three of which came from the Book Depository. According to that consultant, there was between a 25 and 50 percent chance that a fourth shot came from the grassy knoll. These findings of the consultant, particularly in light of the considerable evidence that strongly indicated a total of only three shots had been fired and that they probably all came from the rear, were patently insufficient to deter the Committee from its likely lone assassin assessment. Still, the Committee suggested that the consultant might make further studies and consult with other experts and, if appropriate, return to the Committee with additional evidence.

What followed had all the attributes of a Hollywood B-scenario. On December 18, 1978, the very day that the Committee met in executive session to finalize its conclusions -- again upholding the single-assassin theory, the acoustics consultant, now joined by two additional experts with impressive backgrounds, actually interrupted the Committee's meeting. At figuratively (and almost literally) 11:59 p.m. in the life of the Committee, these three experts presented additional analyses and testimony significantly buttressing a second assassin theory. Though the evidence they presented was extremely technical and complex, the bottom line was unequivocal. It stunned both supporters and opponents of the single-assassin theory. According to these consultants, in addition to three shots having been fired from the sixth floor of the TSBD, there was a 95% probability that a fourth shot was fired from the grassy knoll.

This new "evidence" hit Washington like a bombshell. By the next day, the press learned of this startling development and the Committee came under increased pressure. Ten days later, as its charter drew to a close, the Committee voted, and by a split vote it reversed its preliminary position regarding a conspiracy as expressed in the Report's first draft. The acoustics report was indisputably the cause for the Committee's about-face.

Still pursuing my keen interest in this whole affair, I later interviewed former Congressman Bob Edgar who in his own dissent to the Report and subsequently to me underscored the importance of the acoustic evidence to the final vote of his Committee. Likewise, another member of the Committee, former Congresswoman (now Los Angeles Supervisor), Yvonne Burke, who even aside from the acoustics report still harbors serious qualms about the Warren Commission's lone assassin position, acknowledged to me in a 1992 meeting that the persuasive nature of the acoustics analysis was the main cause for the majority's action. Similarly, Congressman (now Senator) Chris Dodd, writing a separate report, emphasized the potent effect of the acoustics data. He noted his earnest efforts to find "holes" in the accompanying testimony of the acoustics experts, and he concluded that he could not find any serious flaws from a layman's vantage point. Nonetheless, with keen prescience, he called for further analysis and review of the acoustics data before the Committee closed its books.

The language of the Report itself reflects the strain on the decision-makers. At times, its findings are inconsistent with its conclusions. Significantly, the Committee's "high probability" second-gunman finding, in conjunction with its other findings, makes it axiomatic that such a gunman, firing from the grassy knoll, missed hitting anyone or anything. The Committee Report, enigmatically, failed to make such a finding. Furthermore, it, like the Warren Commission, did not conduct trajectory experiments from the grassy knoll (as they did from the TSBD). Had it done so, it would have almost certainly concluded that a second gunman not only didn't hit anyone from that site, but he could not have done so; and he would have instantly known any such effort would have been futile.

Rush to Judgment - 1978-79 Version

Paradoxically, the Committee, in closing its books with its formalized Report issued in January 1979, criticized the Warren Commission because it presented its conclusions in too definitive a fashion. At the same time, cognizant of the troubled feeling of Congressman Dodd and others that so much weight was being given to the acoustics opinions without additional input, it added a telling recommendation. It urged that both the National Institute of Law Enforcement and Criminal Justice of the Department of Justice, along with the National Science Foundation, study the principles of acoustics in relation to the materials available in the JFK assassination and report their respective analyses.

In effect, the Committee passed the buck in regard to an arcane science which none of its members purported to comprehend, let alone master. In doing so, it was confronted with what experienced lawyers are all too familiar. Interestingly, the issues in our society and, more particularly many of those presented in the courts, are so complex that the average citizen or juror cannot hope to understand them without assistance. Thus enters the expert -- "the-man-from-out-of-town-with-a-briefcase." So important have they become to our legal process, that most controversies in court in this day and age involve expert testimony. Each side arms itself. Courts and juries, even with this assistance, are usually baffled or frustrated. This is especially true when experts for each side disagree, which is almost always the case. In such situations, courts and jurors frequently "split the difference" or simply ignore all expert testimony.

In the Kennedy assassination probe, unfortunately, some things were not simplistic. There could be no splitting the difference or ignoring the experts if the aim was to have a rational resolution of the controversy. Once the acoustics issue was raised, there was no way it could be resolved without an in-depth analysis of this relatively new science. But expert testimony can not be taken at face value; other experts may have a different view that is just as, or more, valid. The Committee, however, primarily because of time inhibitions, allowed for no contrary testimony or evidence before rendering a verdict. Rush to judgment.

The Committee's acoustics analysis did not lie dormant. In the years after 1979, others looked into the data and study that convinced the House Committee to abandon the lone-assassin position. The trepidation of Congressman Dodd came to fruition when, almost two years later, after it was directed to undertake a study by the Department of Justice, the Technical Service Division of the FBI released its review of the acoustic data and study presented to the Committee. It boldly challenged the Committee's experts, asserted that there was no scientific evidence that anyone fired a gunshot from the grassy knoll or that the police recording contained any gunshot sounds or even any noises that came from Dealey Plaza. The "two-gunmen" finding of the Committee, the FBI Report pronounced, was "invalid."

Then another salvo zeroed in on the Committee's acoustic findings. This even more thorough review came from the Committee on Ballistic Acoustics of the prestigious National Research Council (of the National Academy of Science). This 12-man committee was composed of highly qualified professors of leading American universities and heads of national, private laboratories. In 1982, that NRC committee, in a wide-ranging and comprehensive report stated:

> "The acoustic analyses [relied upon by the House Committee] do not demonstrate that there was a grassy knoll shot, and in particular there is no acoustic basis for the claim of 95% probability of such a shot.

> The acoustic impulses attributed to gunshots were recorded about one minute after the President had been shot and the motorcade had been instructed to go to the hospital.
>
> Therefore, reliable acoustic data do not support a conclusion that there was a second gunman."

Not a single member of the NRC Committee believed that there was a grassy knoll shot.

The results of these studies in 1980 and 1982 were conveyed to members of the House Committee. According to the Justice Department, it continued to track and review all information that was brought to its attention on this subject for the next six years. Thus, in 1988, the Department formally replied to the House Judiciary Committee as requested by the House Committee almost ten years before. (This document, strangely, was only made available to the public by resort to the Freedom of Information Act). In its formal response, the Justice Department (by William Weld, later Governor of Massachusetts) cited and approved the FBI and NRC findings and concluded that since there was no persuasive criticism of these studies or support for a conspiracy theory in the Kennedy (and M.L. King) assassination, further investigation, in the absence of new evidence, was unwarranted.

The final coup de grace to the critics was seemingly delivered in 1992. The six principal participants in the treatment of Kennedy at Parkland Hospital, and the examination of his body at the Naval Medical Center in Maryland after the assassination - whose testimony was crucial to the Warren Commission's conclusions - point-by-point publicly spoke out. For the first time they denounced the numerous and oft-repeated contentions of the Commission's critics.

Stating that he was breaking a 29-year self-imposed public silence, one of the two chief pathologists conducting the autopsy of Kennedy, Dr. James Humes said he was "tired of being beaten upon by people who are supremely ignorant of the scientific facts of the President's death." He concluded in 1992, as he did in 1963, that

> "We proved at the autopsy table that President Kennedy was struck from above and behind by the fatal shot. The pattern of the entrance and exit wounds in the skull proves it, and if we stayed here until hell freezes over, nothing will change this proof. It happens 100 times out of 100, and I will defend it until I die. This is the essence of our autopsy, and it is supreme ignorance to argue any other scenario. This is a law of physics and it is foolproof - absolutely, unequivocally, and without question. The conspiracy buffs have totally ignored this central scientific fact, and everything else is hogwash. There was no interference with our autopsy, and there was no conspiracy to suppress the findings."

He further reasserted that the other bullet that hit Kennedy (the "magic" bullet) was also the same one that struck Connally and it was fired from above and behind. Both he and the other pathologist conducting the autopsy, Dr. J. T. Boswell, concurred that their examination and findings left "no doubt" as to these vital conclusions.

At the same time, four physicians who actually treated the dying President at Parkland Hospital also spoke out to the editors of the Journal of the American Medical Association:

> "Nothing we observed [they concluded] contradicts the autopsy finding that the bullets were fired from above and behind by a high-velocity rifle."

One other doctor, who assisted in the last steps of the tracheotomy on Kennedy, believed otherwise; he based his opinion primarily upon the Zapruder film which showed that Kennedy's head lurched backwards when the lethal bullet hit him. This doctor admitted, however, that he had no expertise in ballistics, pathology or physics.

As a lawyer and a Virgo, I would generally prefer that a final investigative body put together and make order out of these strange peregrinations in the investigations of the Kennedy assassination. The damage, however, has been done; the exploiters of the Dallas tragedy have become unbridled. Any further effort to set the record straight would be illusory. As experienced lawyers know, emotionally-laden cases never reach final judgment outside the courthouse, in the arena of public opinion. Ding-dong is our destiny. Still, a consensus would be healthy. Respect for facts remains an essential in a civilized society. This despite a 1991 report in the <u>Wall Street Journal</u> (at the height of the critics' attack against the Warren Commission) that, "in a pre-Broadway revival of 'Man of La Mancha,' Don Quixote stirs spontaneous applause from a Washington audience with the line, 'Facts are the enemy of truth.'"

Whatever the view from La Mancha, JFK never intended that to be the legacy of Camelot. In June 1956, it may be recalled, a then largely unknown Senator Kennedy electrified a staid-prone Harvard audience with an eloquent commencement day address. So moved by Kennedy's scholarly words was his colleague, Lyndon B. Johnson, that the Majority Leader not only praised the talk in superlative terms but also inserted it into the <u>Congressional Record</u>. The opening lines of JFK's speech assert: "I can think of nothing more reassuring for all of us than to come again to this institution whose whole purpose is dedicated <u>to the advancement of knowledge and the dissemination of truth</u>." A wholesome respect for facts, he understood, is not only a prerequisite for justice in a legal sense, but in <u>any</u> search for truth.

As singularly traumatic as the JFK assassination miasma is, in and of itself, it is in the long run even more significant and troublesome to the very underpinnings of justice. Lee Harvey Oswald, of course, never went on trial in a legal sense. But, in a larger context, his trial in absentia was the most analyzed and detailed examination of a crime in world history. Tens of thousands investigated it; hundreds of thousands analyzed it; millions viewed and read about it -- and the world gave its verdict.

The Warren Commission's Report had its weaknesses. Still, in light of certain incontestable facts, its basic conclusions are unassailable. But most people, including those exposed to many of the facts, continue to doubt if not outright reject the Report's conclusions. They continue to insist upon a conspiracy, to cling to a grassy knoll, to ignore what almost all experts call scientific facts. Why, and what does it mean?

We have long known of the prejudices of the community -- how we judge others, different than ourselves, more harshly. For most of this nation's history a black man accused of a violent crime against a white person could hardly expect or receive a just trial in much of the country. Leo Frank's plight and lynching in the 1913 backwoods of Georgia was pre-ordained. Sacco and Vanzetti in the elite Bay State in the 1920s may have been guilty, but their trial was a travesty. And the Rodney King beating indictments in Simi Valley, California in 1992, with the attendant video, demanded guilty verdicts, as did the incomparable O.J. trial in Los Angeles three years later. In both courthouses, however, juries refused to burden themselves with incontrovertible facts. Justice in all these cases wasn't merely blind, it was barely comatose.

But each of those infamous results was bottomed on racial or ethnic considerations and, thus, while hardly condonable is explicable. The JFK/Oswald matter had none of these undertones. Thus when Americans overwhelmingly scorn facts in favor of pre-conditioned concepts of conspiracy, what message does this send? The answer may be what savvy lawyers have always understood in their more mundane practices: if you can move the decision-maker's eye off the ball, you can cause the emotive component of his rational apparatus to turn his thoughts away from salient facts and simply go awry. This, it appears, is what I would term "realegalism." And it is the enduring lesson of the JFK assassination investigation. It is, unfortunately, hardly a passing phenomenon.

Chapter 18.

Extra! Extra! The World's Not Fair

World War II had ended about a year before. The country, shaking off a recession, was bustling toward new economic horizons. American values, however, had returned for the most part to those that had prevailed before the war. Women returned to being homemakers; Rosie the Riveter disappeared, not to emerge again for decades. Jim Crow, after a brief sojourn, came back as heavy as ever. Boston, however, had never much gone in for race bigotry. At least on the surface. Perhaps this enlightenment was because the descendants of Harriet Beecher Stowe and William Lloyd Garrison continued to be heard. Or perhaps it was due to the fact that the Hub of the Universe, having but two percent of its population black, could easily "afford" to be benignly tolerant. It even could have been because the blacks were benign -- they "knew their place." The Italians fought the Irish and the Irish beat up on the Jews; everyone, however, seemed to leave the "colored" alone in Boston in the immediate years after the war.

I was in my junior year at the Latin School. Each day after school I would rush to work, selling newspapers outside of South Station, then the most heavily used commuter railway terminal in the country. I had been doing that since before the start of World War II. My father had done the same thing almost thirty years before. Actually, I did not simply sell newspapers. Four or five kids, ages 11 to 14, worked for me at nearby "stands." They hustled for the going wage of 85 cents per day (plus tips) for 2-1/2 hours' work. Of course, I might pay them a bit more if they exceeded the "quota" for that stand; but they had to sell the minimum to keep their jobs. I was aligned with management at a very early age.

I was also naive. One day I did something that hadn't been done at South Station by anyone before, although I didn't know that. I hired a black boy to sell papers at one of "my" stands. He was about twelve; cheerful, good-looking, intelligent (he made change almost as fast as I could), and a hustler in the best sense of the word. I put Josh on a stand that had, day-in and day-out for years, sold approximately 110 newspapers. (The price had just been raised to five cents, or 1.4 cents profit each.) On Josh's very first day, I noted his knack for selling papers: fast, courteous, observant, and a pleasant barker. He sold almost 110 papers that day. Many of his customers seemed surprised, taken aback to see this new paper boy. A couple I recognized went past him and bought their evening papers from some other boy at another stand, 15 or 20 yards away.

For the next few days, Josh's sales fell. By the end of the week, they were less than 100. I went out of my way to see what the problem was. Josh was doing everything right. But people who for years had bought at that stand walked or scampered right past him, seemingly oblivious to his entreaties. After another week, still doing everything right -- indeed, desperately doubling his efforts -- his sales continued to plummet. Three weeks later, he was selling less than an average of 75 papers daily. I was actually beginning to lose money.

I also began to lose my naivete, but not yet my determination. I stuck with Josh for another month. His sales stabilized, but never rose above 80 a day. There was nothing I could do; nothing he could do. We couldn't re-color his skin; and we couldn't stop the commuters from racing to the next stand. We kids couldn't change the world. Moreover, I couldn't afford to continue to lose money; worse, the powers that be -- the publishers -- were threatening to take away "my" stand unless I brought sales back to normal. I had to let Josh go. Martyrdom and survival do not go hand in hand. I was now, at 15, a confounded kid. He, at 12, may have already become wise to the world.

*****

A quarter of a century later, in 1971, I was a successful lawyer, a partner in an old-line law firm, ensconced in finely appointed, fashionable offices high up in the sky, three thousand miles away from the cold, windy, newsboy corners of South Station. Everything had changed, and nothing had changed.

Almost all lawyers are employers. Even sole practitioners usually have secretaries and/or office help. The larger and more modern firms employ two to three times the number of support personnel as they have attorneys. Partners also, of course, employ lesser gods -- salaried associates. Lawyers are treated in law like any other business when it comes to hiring practices. Experience has shown that lawyers, conservative by nature, are not trailblazers in the pursuit of equal employment opportunity in their own practices. In fact, from coast to coast, law firms, until the past couple of decades, notoriously had adopted and adhered to the most restricted covenants that ran throughout the land.

Thus, for many lawyers and law firms, the enactment of the numerous and far-reaching fair employment statutes was near traumatic. Many greeted these measures in much the same manner as one reacts to word of a terminal illness: first avoidance, then anger, followed by denial, then bargaining, and finally, resignation. The issue of hiring minority and women attorneys confronted many practitioners with difficult moral and professional problems.

Lawyers responded along predictable lines. About a third of them readily supported the revolution; another third originally were opposed. Fortunately, the usual pivotal third, often reluctantly, joined the forward movement toward equal opportunity. When it came to a showdown, my partners were no less divided philosophically than the nation. Very few, however, were or remained outspoken opponents; and the majority of them were realists and accepted the inevitable. Still, in 1970, when the issue came down to making our first offer to a female law school graduate, some further foot-dragging was not easily ended.

Rare was the voice among us, however, who raised the hackneyed hokum that women were not meant to be lawyers or that they couldn't "mix." Seldom did we hear the canard that they would not be able to take the strain or devote the long hours necessary to achieve success. Hardly ever was it mentioned, even in the corridors, that the partners would have to watch their vocabularies and clean up their jokes. Ribaldry was declasse.

There was, however, one disturbing point that was raised, quietly but repeatedly. It resurrected for me the specter of Josh, selling newspapers and catering to the customers. One partner cogently argued that even if a woman attorney could, in the course of time and through the dint of hard work and topnotch product, win the confidence of most of our existing clients, the nature of our firm and long-range success required something more difficult. In the ever-increasing, competitive legal field, he reminded us that, aside from being good lawyers, most of us have to be or become good business-getters. Otherwise, we starve. The quick-moving business world is easily enticed to go to the next legal shop down the street. As baleful as it may sound, he said, there is something about the "ole boy" network -- it brings in clients.

There was, I had to confess, merit to that argument, despite its Catch-22 logic. A law partnership is not an eleemosynary institution. Partners must produce, and most of them are expected to bring business -- clients -- into the firm. If women do not have the connections and aren't in the clubs, don't play handball (even if they can play hardball), and if most of the business world has a hang-up about women-as-lawyers, what is the future of the firm, rang the query. Little to none, was the glum answer from one or more of the larger offices. Whatever changes may be in the making, it was said, they simply won't come in time to stave off the inevitable result of cutting off the spigot.

Yes, the experience of South Station was edifying. Its teachings were not, however, inevitable. I was no longer a 15-year-old helpless romantic. I was a successful lawyer, allied to the so-called "Establishment." The barriers to economic opportunity were coming down nonetheless with its help. The power of the law -- both as a moral tutor and cast-iron cop -- was steering society in a bold, new direction. With intelligence and a little luck, we could make the transition successfully; we need not lose our "stand." Not all of us thought this through in the same manner; nor were all convinced. Yet, when it came to the showdown, we voted to make the offer. Many acted enthusiastically, others reluctantly; but in the end, none opposed.

If the period of influx and integration of women as major players in the practice of law was not the bar's finest hour, it is one that lawyers, on the whole, can take a measure of pride in. Lawyers have, by their own conduct in recent years, much to be ashamed of; but the role of women in the profession does not belong on that list.

Granted that there presently exists discrimination that should not be brooked, and recognizing that some feminist leaders can never be satisfied, still the gains made by and acceptance of women in the law have been very encouraging. In less than thirty years, the number of women bar admittees has risen from single-digit percentages to one-half of all newly "ordained" attorneys. Their selection to the bench has been equally impressive. Now, with the advent of time, they are beginning to enter into the sanctum sanctorum of most large firms in accelerating numbers. Resistance in other areas of society was far more pronounced than it proved to be in the stodgy law business.

* * * * *

Even among those often identified as the best and the brightest, there appeared stout pockets of resistance to women's demands for the right to become part of the action. One such skirmish occurred, coincidentally, just a few short weeks after my firm, as discussed above, opened itself up to the latter part of the Twentieth Century. For the prior two or three years, the pressure had been mounting toward and within the Harvard Club of Southern California that it should be in the vanguard of liberated men. The Radcliffe alumnae, much smaller in numbers in the Los Angeles area than their Harvard counterparts, had urged that the Radcliffe graduates be admitted to the Harvard Club.

Since in Cambridge, the two schools had for years integrated their teaching curricula and were on the verge of adopting a mutual admissions policy, the merger of the two groups seemed sensible. Actually, the Cliffies wanted to be able to belong to the Harvard Club but keep their separate club at the same time. I supported the proposed admissions policy to the Club. As president of the Club at the time, I took it upon myself, moreover, to facilitate this liberalized membership policy.

I did not expect too much difficulty in getting approval of the Board of Directors. There were no economic consequences to the Club's broadening its base. If anything, it would likely add to the Club's coffers; and, or course, these new members were more likely to take an active role in and support the Club's programs.

To my surprise, the opposition to a unisex Harvard Club was formidable. To some, admittedly a distinct minority, my "liberalism" on this issue was anathema. Highly intelligent and otherwise progressive and hardworking members for whom the very name "Harvard" commanded veneration, voiced their opposition in strong though properly restrained tones. Allowing women to participate fully in the operation of the Club was to some the equivalent of tearing up the hallowed grass and cutting down the ancient trees in The Yard.

The crux of their position generally came down to what might on the surface be labeled "chauvinism." If we allow them in, they will take over the place. They will run the show. We were repeatedly told that these women, particularly the younger ones, had an agenda that was different from Harvard's. It was the feminist program, they were convinced. The ideas of Betty Friedan and Jane Fonda. "Bye, bye," the Harvard Club as we knew it, they groaned.

I patiently responded to their arguments. I pointed out that neither Friedan nor Fonda were even Radcliffe graduates, and their ideas would hardly interfere with the Club's program or purpose. Furthermore, I said, it is ridiculous to believe that Radcliffe graduates, whatever their position regarding the feminist movement, were about to stage a putsch and turn this bastion of decorum into a liberation front.

It was probably not my arguments that convinced any of the opposition. If they were convinced of anything, it was solely the inevitability that the integration would come, if not immediately, soon. Beleaguered, most of the curmudgeons resigned themselves to the facts, with an "*apres moi la deluge*" attitude. A few months later, the formalities were completed. Radcliffe alumnae became members of "our" club.

Over the next sixteen years, although I attended a good many of the Harvard-Radcliffe functions, I ceased being active in its internal operations. There was no question, however, that the Club's activities not only increased in number, but improved in quality and interest to the alumni(ae). Membership rose to unprecedented heights and the Club seemed, at least from a distance, to have a new vitality. The experiment, I concluded with a sense of pride, had succeeded.

Then, one day in October 1987, I received my monthly Harvard-Radcliffe newsletter. Along with write-ups on coming programs, it had attached the usual couple of "Flyers," special events or notices of one kind or another. One such attached flyer read:

"THEY JUST AREN'T LISTENING TO YOU!"
For the past 7 years, your elected representatives in Washington and
Sacramento have willfully ignored your wishes and abused your trust...

The Iran-Contra Scandal
The nomination of Robert Bork to the
Supreme Court
Abortion rights restricted

You don't have to take it anymore!

You don't have to settle for the "lesser of evils"
in the 1988 elections.

YOU CAN TAKE CONTROL!

On October 14, you'll learn about a proven
strategy that will mean real changes in 1988 and
beyond.

"THE FEMINIZATION OF POWER
National Campaign Tour

Wednesday, October 14, 1987, 8:00 p.m.
Scottish Rite Auditorium
4357 Wilshire Boulevard, Los Angeles

Featuring
ELEANOR SMEAL
President, The Fund for the Feminist Majority"

The broadside then went on to explain who to contact to join the "Harvard-Radcliffe group" attending the event. It concluded, "The Fund For the Feminist Majority is not a membership organization. There are no dues. We are a dynamic movement for feminist women and men to gain the political power necessary to effect real change."

I understand that an avalanche of protests reached Club officers because of the flyer; the Club had to apologize in its next newsletter. I suppose I had a special duty to apologize to those curmudgeons of yesteryear to whom I had given assurances that their fears were entirely unjustified. Unfortunately, most of them have since, in the Yale phrase, "gone from here to eternity."

* * * * *

On the very day that I heard that the Harvard-Radcliffe Club had formally apologized, my firm's partnership, without any fanfare whatsoever, voted in its first female full partner. For the requisite years, she had earned the respect of every partner in the firm. I had no doubt that in time she would come to be recognized as one of the best attorneys in the firm, and this prediction came to pass. She earned her stripes, however, the old-fashioned way.

Chapter 19.

The World Of Our Fathers -- Ready-Mix Justice

For more than two hundred years, American government has been founded upon the deliberate, diffused distribution of power, as Madison propounded and prophesied in The Federalist Papers (#10). Yet, as Hamilton noted (#78), in this division of constitutional power among the three branches of government, the judiciary, in theory, is the least potent:

> "Whoever attentively considers the different departments of power must perceive that, in a government in which they are separated from each other, the judiciary, from the nature of its functions, will always be the least dangerous to the political rights of the Constitution; because it will be least in a capacity to annoy or injure them. The executive not only dispenses the honours, but holds the sword of the community. The legislature not only commands the purse, but

prescribes the rules by which the duties and rights of every citizen are to be regulated. The judiciary, on the contrary, has no influence over either the sword or the purse; no direction either of the strength or of the wealth of the society; and can take no active resolution whatever. It may truly be said to have neither FORCE nor WILL, but merely judgment; and must ultimately depend upon the aid of the executive arm even for the efficacy of its judgments.

This simple view of the matter suggests several important consequences. It proves incontestably that the judiciary is beyond comparison the weakest of the three departments of power..."

Hamilton scarcely envisioned that the courts frequently would come to exercise the final and dominant power in the most important spheres of both private rights and public affairs. It may be the "least dangerous" branch, but the judiciary is no longer the least powerful. Still, in the final analysis, its power is based almost entirely upon faith and myth. The people must believe in its independence and integrity -- an article of faith. Judges must be a notch above most of the rest of us in the pursuit of power -- a necessary myth.

Lawyers are supposed to be guardians of that faith and myth. We interact with the judiciary so as to ensure that both will abide the straight and narrow. That is what all my formal training taught me. My environment did likewise. My father was a practicing attorney for ten years. (He was my only relative who was, save for my godfather -- "Eddie" something or other -- whom I had never met.) While my dad was too wise and knowledgeable about Boston politics to be an uncritical adherent of this myth, despite himself he looked upon the judiciary with an awe shared by most of his generation; he undoubtedly instilled some of that reverence in me.

The years and my experience since, of course, have buffeted that faith and myth. The typical attorney is treated as a mere underling by most judges. This is hardly surprising. Judges wield such power that they reign like virtual monarchs holding court. While very many judges earn respect, almost all of them command it. But in recent years, in particular, in concert with lawyers and society generally, the judiciary is increasingly courting "a long farewell...to greatness" and respect.

In some measure this is because nationwide media revelations of criminal and otherwise dishonorable activities by judges tend to suggest that such conduct occurs more now than in earlier times. A multitude of other factors have come to undermine the judiciary -- many such wounds being self-inflicted. There is a traditional but increasing tendency of judges to favor "hometown" litigants or "club" members. All attorneys can testify to "cow country" justice, the unbalanced treatment or heavy-handedness accorded "visiting" litigants. Some of this, of course, is sour grapes, but so pronounced are the complaints of this hometown bias, that they cannot easily be dismissed. The impression, in any event, is undeniable. Similarly, the favoritism that judges display to friendly attorneys, members of the "club", those instrumental in having brought about their appointments to the bench and likely to be helpful in promoting them, is another stigma recognized by most practitioners.

This diminution in esteem also results, in part, from the huge numerical expansion in judgeships. These positions need to be filled by drawing from an available pool which is, unfortunately, reduced by many of the most able and qualified attorneys refusing to accept such positions. These lawyers often decline to be considered because of the relatively meager compensation presently accorded judges, compared to both judges' earnings historically and to what attorneys in private practice now earn. Furthermore, the expansion in the numbers of judgeships reduces the distinction and honor of the position, to some degree. The former exclusivity of this inner club -- and its attendant prestige -- was a magnet for enticing the qualified. That lure is less now than ever before.

One recent phenomenon is even more ominous for the continued vitality of our judicial system. Since the 1980's, many judges in California and elsewhere have had a penchant for seeking appointment to the court and, perhaps with aforethought but certainly soon thereafter, in a matter of but a few years, they resign from the bench. Why? Most of these judges who prematurely resign do so to make more money, not only in private practice but as private judges earning as much as $500 an hour. Thus, there is in the making a privatization of our legal system where well-heeled litigants can have their cases heard with dispatch by a judge of their own choosing -- unlike the rest of the populace who must wait in line and have the judge next in line hear their cases with or without the approval of the parties. This not only creates a two-tiered "justice" system, but these judges -- the holiest of the holy -- undermine the vital respect and prestige of all judges and the entire system is put in jeopardy.

Most of all, however, the reduced respect accorded the judiciary relates to a perception that judges wrongly employ their own personal prejudices and beliefs in ascertaining "The Law," perceiving their subjective ideas of good and evil to be the objective equivalent of what the community does -- or should -- deem wise. That judges are so viewed is hardly surprising; such a view is preordained. First, judges, being human, tend to personalize disputations. Second, our society has religiously invested judges with the appearance of piety and the unfettered power of philosopher-kings. We have given our courts an irrevocable license to be society's surrogates.

In so fulfilling this role, of necessity, judges politicize and (more dangerously) personalize their writ. When they, inevitably, make their political and personal prejudices obvious, and painful to many, segments of society revolt. Debates about strict and loose "construction," "conservative" or "liberal" approaches, making or applying "The Law" cloud reality. Power manifests itself throughout the spectrum of law, and in every shade of subtlety.

An attorney, even if he or she wanted, could not change the "system". He must at least appear to adjust himself to the institution of which he is a part. The lawyer exists to curry the favor, not the displeasure, of the court. He adheres to the accepted "proprieties" for sound reasons: an implausible or a knowingly unavailing attack on the actions of a court can only further undermine the myth, exacerbating rather than ameliorating the overall problem. Such "offensiveness", moreover, is likely to prejudice further the lawyer and his client in the pending case (and perhaps even future cases) before the same judge.

For these reasons, most lawyers seldom attack, at least directly, the known prejudices of the judge. Lawyers rarely raise the issue directly that a judge should recuse himself or be overruled because he has an unwarranted personal predisposition against a litigant's cause (or the litigant or his counsel personally) and that the judge's actions might be affected by these prejudices. But there are exceptions. Sometimes the bias is so blatant that the attack is unavoidable.

One such instance arose, unexpectedly, in 1968; I was really only on the sidelines. Kyle Brown, a young associate in the firm, had been practicing labor law for only a couple of years but was ready and itching to try a case by himself. When the right kind came along, a typical management-union clash, an unfair labor practice claim before the NLRB, I assigned it to him. He prepared and handled the case himself, with scarcely any help from me. After the first day of the hearing, Kyle returned to the office bemoaning what he considered to be the marked bias against our employer-client by the Administrative Law Judge, E. David Davis (who had been sent down from San Francisco to preside on this case). I had never heard of that judge, but that made no difference. I immediately rejected Kyle's suggestion that he make a motion the next day to Judge Davis to have the judge remove himself from the case because of his prejudicial remarks.

"Stan, this guy is so biased in favor of unions, it's incredible. He doesn't even try to hide it! We're dead in the water with that donkey," said Brown. He went on to relate a number of off-the-record comments by Judge Davis that surely showed a hidebound bias against management in general and our client in particular.

While I did not doubt Kyle's account of convoluted justice in the making, I continued to brush off his suggestion to move to have the judge take himself off the case. "Kyle, you're naive. It's not done. I never did it, and, in ten years of practice, I never heard of anyone else doing it. Even after trial and judgment, hardly any judge is found to be prejudiced by the Board in Washington. No way. And what he said is not even on the record. Disheartened, Kyle left to prepare for his next day's trial.

When Kyle returned from the hearing the following afternoon, he was beside himself. He announced that Judge Davis' one-sided antics that day were beyond the pale. "He practically told me that our client lacks credibility, simply because the company opposes unionization. He keeps interjecting my cross-examination, giving the General Counsel's witnesses a blueprint for answering my questions, completely undermining the effectiveness of my examination. The hearing's a charade with that turkey running it," Kyle groused.

"Make up your mind, tiger," I flippantly replied to Kyle's bitterness. "He's either a donkey or a turkey, but he can't be both."

"Look, generalissimo, I'm not playing patsy to him or you. I've got him on the record and I've ordered an overnight copy of the transcript. Tomorrow morning you can read it. When you do, you'll change your mind. That dingo's got to go!"

Sure enough, when I read portions of the reporter's transcript early the next day, Judge Davis' statements throughout betrayed a brazen partiality in support of the union. He unabashedly expressed a favoritism other judges assiduously hide. Kyle, I knew, was a crackerjack lawyer, and I was compelled to agree with him that he should move to have the judge disqualify himself. However, I conceded with a rather smug exhortation, "Okay, Don Quixote mount your Rosinante, and do the bastard in!"

Soon thereafter, Kyle made his daring motion. An irritated but now judicially subdued Judge Davis predictably took the motion "under submission," indicating that he would allow the Board in Washington, D.C. to rule on it "in due time." He continued the hearing, giving official indifference to the motion. A few days later, the hearing was concluded. A month later, he filed his decision, finding for the union. The following month Kyle appealed that decision to the NLRB in Washington, and raised again the motion to have Judge Davis disqualified based upon prejudice.

While the appeal in that matter was pending, I was preparing a far more important NLRB case. A major labor dispute between my clients, the leading asphalt and ready-mix concrete producers in Southern California and the Operating Engineers union had culminated in a lengthy hard-fought strike. We were eventually successful in obtaining a court injunction against the union. The real legal battle, however, would follow -- could our position be upheld by the NLRB in a full-blown trial before an Administrative Law Judge? The issues were quite technical. The Regional Director of the NLRB had issued a complaint against the union; the rub was that he had not sought a complete remedy that would give my clients the full relief to which they felt entitled and which they needed because of the union's wrongful actions. My task was, therefore, first to support and prove the General Counsel's complaint against the union, and then to turn around and convince the judge that the General Counsel had not gone far enough. In a word, I was seeking the whole enchilada.

I had been working on the case for months. Kyle, a few weeks before trial, had started to assist me while his bout with Judge Davis wended its way through the appeals process.

Together we spent endless hours preparing our numerous witnesses and developing our legal theories. The shape and direction of the industry for years to come seemed likely to rest, to a considerable extent, upon our success or failure.

On the morning the trial was to commence in the federal courthouse, we met with our clients and witnesses in my office for a final briefing. I was asked who the judge would be. I explained that NLRB procedure was such that we would not know the judge's identity until the trial actually began, as he or she is assigned, hush-hush from the NLRB offices in either San Francisco or Washington. Kyle, in a bite-your-tongue manner, snarled, "Let's hope it isn't Davis!" He then briefly explained his remark. I assured our clients that since there was a pool of 25 judges in San Francisco and many more in Washington from which a judge would be selected, the chances of getting Davis were so slim that we could practically dismiss the possibility. We then all took off for the courthouse.

We took seats in the courtroom, our clients in the rear, Kyle and I at the charging parties' table, the union counsel at another table, and attorneys for the NLRB at their separate sideboard -- some six or seven attorneys in all. At the appointed hour of 9:30 a.m., in strode the judge, a large and courtly-looking man. I looked at him without any particular reaction; I had never seen him before, Kyle spotted him and turned green. He exclaimed in my ear, "Stan, that's Davis!"

I immediately realized the predicament that we were in. There were still a few minutes remaining before the trial would open. The judge took his seat on the bench and began looking around at counsel. I had no doubt that he was sizing up -- and probably down -- Kyle, and, by extension, me. I turned to my clients and asked them to step outside the courtroom where I wanted to talk to them. Kyle and I then went to another room with our clients, and I explained the dilemma. I told them that Judge Davis was probably -- indeed, undoubtedly -- prejudiced against us because Kyle (with my blessing) had challenged his fairness in a recent, still undecided, case. I explained to the clients that their rights easily could be prejudiced by our representing them, indicating that the asphalt and ready-mix concrete industry might be ill-served by our continuing on the case. They had, I said, the alternative of asking me to seek a continuance and getting new counsel or of allowing Davis to stay on the case despite probable, or at least possible, prejudice. After talking amongst themselves, they told me that they would take the risk of keeping us on the case and that we should proceed. After assuring myself that that was indeed our clients' wish and that all the facts and implications were clear to them, we returned to the courtroom and sat ready to put on our case.

Judge Davis opened the proceedings by introducing himself and making a few preliminary remarks. He then asked all counsel to make their appearances on the record, eyeing me carefully, I thought uneasily. That accomplished, he announced that he wanted all counsel to approach the bench. He pointedly was going off the record. I whispered to Kyle, "He's going to raise the fact that you prejudiced him. The worm turns, friend!" Kyle nodded, ruefully, in agreement.

As counsel surrounded the judge, he stated, without looking at me in particular, "Gentlemen, I may be prejudiced in this case, or some people may think I am prejudiced." Kyle and I winked knowingly, prepared, we thought, for what the judge would say.

He continued, "I do not believe I am prejudiced, however. Notwithstanding the fact that I am the godfather of one of the counsel in this case, I think I can look at it objectively."

All the lawyers, bewildered, looked at each other. Whose godfather was he? Judge Davis then went on, "Mr. Tobin's father and I were boyhood friends. When Mr. Tobin was born, I was chosen as his godfather. We haven't seen or communicated with each other since, although I have heard about him from others on the Board. Under these circumstances, if you want me to excuse myself from the case, I will certainly do so."

All of us surrounding the bench, myself especially, were stunned. Kyle was in a state of utter disbelief, totally flabbergasted. Ringing in his ears was my recent battle cry to "get the bastard!" But the truth of the matter was that I did not know E. (for Eddie) David Davis from J. Edgar Hoover. I vaguely remembered that my father had told me that I had a godfather who worked for the NLRB, but that was long before I practiced in this area. I was innocent, I swear.

The other attorneys, aware of Davis' professional prejudice, or fearful of his personal wrath, or uncertain as to his brood, "graciously" waived any objection. To an observer, all this was like a scene from a "C" rated movie out of Tinseltown. (I suppose I should have cried out, "Daddy!") To Kyle and me, it was more like the Twilight Zone.

* * * *

The trial began. By the second day, the issue was joined. The General Counsel and I had fairly proven the narrow allegations of the complaint. Now I wanted to offer testimony that would expand the scope of the hearing, enabling my clients to obtain durable relief. The General Counsel, however, along with the union, of course, vigorously resisted my attempted anschluss. Each of us argued the legal aspects of my admittedly novel maneuver. Judge Davis listened patiently, though with some skepticism, to my legal rationale. It was Friday noon when we finished our arguments and Davis began to sum up the issue I had raised. Surprisingly, he seemed uncertain as to how to rule, whether to permit me to put on the additional evidence so as to expand the complaint or to deny my motion, allow the union to defend itself on the limited reach of the complaint, and then adjourn the hearing. While wavering, he glanced at the clock and then suggested that it seemed like a good idea to recess for the weekend; we would reconvene Monday morning.

That evening, a call came from the East Coast. Dad.

"Stan, you'll never guess who I got a call from," he said effusively. "Try me," I replied dryly. My father, understandably, couldn't have been more delighted by the wondrous turn of events had he won the Irish Sweepstakes. He went on to extol Davis' extolling me. He told me how close they had been in their younger days, and how Davis would do anything for him. I began to sniff a delicate -- dangerous -- situation in the making. I pried, trying to assure myself, judiciously so to speak, that my father was not extending paternalism beyond pride or pale. His telling me in keen summary the critical issues that were left dangling at the hearing that day did not reassure me that the old buddy system was not stirring.

"Listen, Dad," I said wearily, "I realize you guys have a great bond between you. Swell, but don't call your chips in as it relates to me or my case. Please, no tricks; no treats."

"But you don't understand. He owes me one. More than one. I pulled him through law school. We go back together almost 50 years. I don't even have to ask. You understand?"

By this time, I was getting worked up. I didn't want any ready-made justice. "Damn it, Dad. Don't you dare call him back until this case is finished. And if he calls you again, avoid any discussion whatsoever of the case I'm on," adding adamantly, "I mean it!"

"All right, if that's the way you want it," my father said with apparent resignation. "But let me warn you, I remember when we were in law school and during the Thirties, he was one hundred percent pro-union; and from the way he talked on the phone, he's still that way!"

"Tell me," I muttered sarcastically.

On Monday, the trial resumed. Judge Davis announced that he would hear the union's defensive witnesses to the case as limited. But, he added, he still had not decided whether to grant or deny my motion to expand the scope of the testimony and hearing. He was, therefore, taking that "interesting" issue under submission and wanted the parties to send him written briefs on the question within two weeks after the recess, which would begin the next day. If he should then decide to grant the motion to expand the hearing, he said, he would notify the parties and the trial would resume the following month. If he denied the motion, he would routinely issue his decision on the complaint as issued.

Whether intended or not, his ruling had a Solomon-like effect. While he certainly had not decided the issue in my favor, nor even suggested that he would do so, the very fact that he was taking this additional time to decide, and also wanted briefs, unnerved the union. A few days after the recess, I received a telephone call from the union's counsel suggesting the parameters for settlement. After a few days of parleying, we were able to package a deal that gave my clients most of the security they were seeking. The matter having been settled, Judge Davis did not have to either reopen the hearing or render any kind of decision. Justice appeared to have been served.

A postscript: Some months later, and at times over the next few years before his death, Judge Davis and I met and dined together. We never discussed "Kyle's Case." For historical trivia buffs, I note that when "Kyle's Case" was decided by the NLRB (a few months after the asphalt/ready-mix matter was settled), the Board, as expected, in a footnote found it "unnecessary" to reach the issue of whether Judge Davis was wrongfully prejudiced. Still, his prejudices notwithstanding, he had many worthwhile things to say and was a warm and interesting storyteller.

Chapter 20.

"Let Us Raise A Somewhat Loftier Strain" (Virgil)

Through all the years of my practice, I have each holiday season sent greeting cards to clients and friends. By design, they all have had a legal theme. Looking back, I now realize that these cards, changing over time in genre and motif, unconsciously reflect professional passages; they mirror changes in my own shifting mood and outlook. For about a decade, these greeting cards reproduced the sprightly and colorful Spy likenesses of the luminaries of England's bench and bar. Then, for a few transitional years, they portrayed the naturalistic, stern, but uplifting American jury scenes of Winslow Homer and others of the same style. For most of the past twenty years, these cards have been mainly Daumier caricatures -- dour "Men of Justice" figures depicted in an ironic, black-humor vein.

It would be a relief to end these vignettes on the life of the law on an encouraging note. Such would serve the natural desire of both the reader and the writer. The reader seeks to be reassured.

In defiance of what he sees all around him, despite what his senses tell him, he yearns for signs of hope; he forcefully turns his back on despair. By instinct and inclination, this writer has long been a visceral optimist. The Jeremiah is universally rejected, and rejection hurts.

Cognitive dissonance, whatever possible palliative effect it may have on one's private life, however, is counterproductive to professional coping. No one engaged professionally in jurisprudence -- even aside from any idealistic search for justice -- can be blind to current realities. And the pall that hangs over the functioning of the judicial system is now so pronounced, the warnings of pending crisis so clear, that the alarms of Laocoon and cries of Cassandra can be ignored only by those programmed to fail.

The likelihood is that such admonitions will be ignored. It is certainly a legitimate (though unanswered) question that others have advanced: "Does anyone really want 'justice' who is not a total onlooker?" Litigants may assert it; lawyers extol it; judges proclaim it. But if the public is simply an onlooker and otherwise ignores its plight or allows its abuse, whatever remains will be "justice by mistake".

The practice of law has always been a delicate balance. It is a constant tugging between the requirement to maintain professional standards, to be officers of the court, to seek justice; and the need to earn a living, to be business-like. Add to this, are the remains of the old-fashioned notion that lawyers owe a debt to society. What has become ominous, however, is that there is now an apparently unstoppable surge to ignore the less tangible values and adopt the lower standards and become part of the win-at-any-price marketplace.

The perennial onus of bearing "the law's delay, the insolence of office" is now being exacerbated. The growing resort to hucksteri and hustling is appalling. The outrageous fees demanded all but preclude at least half the populace's access to the courts. The self-interest of the professional participants has compromised at least the appearance of impartiality of judges and lawyers. The allowable artifices and permissible papering have turned what is touted as an orderly process into nothing less than an ordeal. The increasingly impersonal relationship between the client and his high-tower, high-falutin counsel further reduces the human hub in the wheel of justice.

In the less hustle-bustle days of yesteryear, when there were far more farmers than lawyers, the bar policed itself with considerably more effectiveness than is the case today. Numbers alone so burden the profession that the informal but effective peer pressures of past generations no longer exist. When members of the bar knew each and every lawyer in town, if not personally, at least by reputation, sleaziness did not escape unnoticed; and shunning, if not outright and immediate discipline, was the likely consequence. Peer watch-dogging in America -- where two-thirds of all the lawyers in the world reside and are turning their profession into a trade -- can no longer have efficacy. Surely, the average practitioner in any metropolitan area in the country has an in-depth knowledge of only a minute percentage of his fellow lawyers. And in cities like New York, where over 70,000 lawyers do-their-thing, the moral influence of the legal community is, at best, ziltch and shibboleth.

Into this cauldron of chaos we must add to the judicial system's woes an ever-more-complex society enacting incrementally complicated laws. These, in turn, entice a burgeoning population to join an inherently litigious one. This hubbub is reigned over by a bench that is now more politicized but less monitored, assisted by a bar that unabashedly equates its privileges with society's rights. At the bottom of this deluge wearily rests a complacent community that manifests increasing symptoms of moral decline.

Indeed, complacency and indifference, more than opposition, undermines the search for justice. The legal system can scarcely breathe soul into society; it generally reflects, rather than restores, the spirit. The mores of our time make reluctant skeptics of us all.

The tragedy of Kitty Genovese, in New York in the Sixties, is less that her killer escaped than that 38 of her neighbors turned a deaf ear to her screams and hellish death. The anguish of the gravely mistreated Elizabeth Steinberg in that same city a generation later was rending enough, but the distancing of the community from her pathos is the mind-boggling crime. The grisly murder of a lonely 14-year-old girl by her high school hoodlum boyfriend in the upper-middle-class town of Milpitas, California, in 1981, was depressing. The unconcerned and accepting attitude of a dozen of his classmates is devastating. It is only in degree that these particular wrenching events made the daily news and that endless other serious injustices completely escape everyone's attention. In such an environment, in such an age, what chance does an esoteric concept called "justice" have to survive, let alone thrive? Surely, however, we are forced to consider that similar questions have been posed repeatedly in other eras in history.

A hundred years ago, Oliver Wendell Holmes, Jr., who was to become the nation's foremost democratic jurist, lamented the trend in the type of lawyering he was witnessing. Lawyers, he bemoaned, were sinking to the level of the times. They were actually "exalt[ing] that most hateful of American words and ideals, 'smartness,' as against dignity of moral feeling and profundity of knowledge." Holmes was railing against the "new gospel" which was insidiously changing a profession founded upon moral dignity into a business resting upon smarts. The current ills and evils of lawyering -- in this Prolonged Time of Trouble -- dwarf those perceived by that Brahmin. That brilliant puritan could scarcely relate to today's Babylon-in-law.

Yet, many years later, though never losing sight of the difficulties of having lawyers heed the dictates of a profession, and still acutely aware of the fragile underpinnings of democracy, Holmes "dreamed" beyond the trials of the times. "The life of the law," he had epically enunciated earlier, "has not been logic; it has been experience." In 1913, after serving on the Supreme Court for over 10 years, he lifted his vision beyond both logic and experience. The transplanted Bostonian, in the florid prose of the Edwardian era, wrote of his dream:

> The other day my dream was pictured to my mind. It was evening. I was walking homeward on Pennsylvania Avenue near the Treasury, and as I looked beyond Sherman's Statue to the west the sky was aflame with scarlet and crimson from the setting sun. But, like the note of downfall in Wagner's opera, below the skyline there came from little globes the pallid discord of the electric lights. And I thought to myself the Gotterdammerung will end, and from those globes clustered like evil eggs will come the new masters of the sky. It is like the time in which we live. But then I remembered the faith that I partly have expressed, faith in a universe not measured by our fears, a universe that has thought and more than thought inside of it, and as I gazed, after the sunset and above the electric lights there shone the stars.

Can we be hopeful for the future as Holmes was at the beginning of the 20th century -- the American Century? Slowly churning are changes in the legal system that could make a difference. Foremost among them is the trend toward arbitration and mediation of legal disputes. While this may beneficially reduce court log jams and drawbacks caused by the adversary process, this will hardly be a panacea; it has downsides. It will compromise due process protections, and help foster a two-tier system of justice, one public, one private. Interestingly, this change will bring us closer to the justice system of continental Europe -- less juries, and a less publicity-prone and lawyer-dominated process. It also moves us in the direction of the Japanese concept of justice -- consensus -- and its anti-litigation component. It remains to be seen whether such "advancements" can thrive in such multi-ethnic soil as will exist in the 21st century in America.

In the years to come other modifications in the process could alleviate some of today's egregious hangups: Turning the hardships and headaches of family distress away from the divorce litigation ordeal toward a socially-oriented, lawyer-limited forum. Reducing the size and scope of juries in some particularly technical and complicated matters; perhaps even specialized business courts. Capping civil punitive awards so that they can be distinguished from criminal penalties and the resultant perversion that has turned the legal process into a dicey Hobson's Choice for most, and a no-lose lottery for many. These, and other important changes and innovations (some now not even being debated), are sure to come about. They will significantly refashion the wiles that lawyers now practice and the ways the system now stumbles along.

Still, as we are at times rightfully reminded, change does not necessarily equate with progress. Yet, it is possible to envision the achievement of our loftier goals because (as Holmes seems to be saying), after all, there were brighter yesterdays. Until then, however, I expect I will continue to send gray Daumier greeting cards, knowing that that Nineteenth Century genius died a pauper, totally blind. He left us, however, with a powerful and everlasting visual legacy that constantly depicts that those in search of justice must overcome cant.